The Hong Kong Economic Policy Studies Series

RETIREMENT PROTECTION:
A PLAN FOR HONG KONG

T0154861

RETIREMENT PROTECTION: A PLAN FOR HONG KONG

Francis T. Lui

Published for
The Hong Kong Centre for Economic Research
The Better Hong Kong Foundation
The Hong Kong Economic Policy Studies Forum
by

City University of Hong Kong Press

First published 1998
Printed in Hong Kong

ISBN 962-937-030-1

Published by
City University of Hong Kong Press
City University of Hong Kong
Tat Chee Avenue, Kowloon, Hong Kong

Internet: http://www.cityu.edu.hk/upress/
E-mail: upress@cityu.edu.hk

The free-style calligraphy on the cover, *qi*, means "elderly" in Chinese.

Contents

Detailed Chapter Contents

Foreword

The key to the economic success of Hong Kong has been a business and policy environment which is simple, predictable and transparent. Experience shows that prosperity results from policies that protect private property rights, maintain open and competitive markets, and limit the role of the government.

The rapid structural change of Hong Kong's economy in recent years has generated considerable debate over the proper role of economic policy in the future. The restoration of sovereignty over Hong Kong from Britain to China has further complicated the debate. Anxiety persists as to whether the pre-1997 business and policy environment of Hong Kong will continue.

During this period of economic and political transition in Hong Kong, various interested parties will be re-assessing Hong Kong's existing economic policies. Inevitably, they will advocate an agenda aimed at altering the present policy making framework to reshape the future course of public policy.

For this reason, it is of paramount importance for those familiar with economic affairs to reiterate the reasons behind the success of the economic system in the past, to identify what the challenges are for the future, to analyze and understand the economy sector by sector, and to develop appropriate policy solutions to achieve continued prosperity.

In a conversation with my colleague Y. F. Luk, we came upon the idea of inviting economists from universities in Hong Kong to take up the challenge of examining systematically the economic policy issues of Hong Kong. An expanding group of economists (The Hong Kong Economic Policy Studies Forum) met several times to give form and shape to our initial ideas. The Hong Kong Economic Policy Studies Project was then launched in 1996 with some 30 economists from the universities in Hong Kong and a few

from overseas. This is the first time in Hong Kong history that a
concerted public effort has been undertaken by academic economists in the territory. It represents a joint expression of our
collective concerns, our hopes for a better Hong Kong, and our faith
in the economic future.

The Hong Kong Centre for Economic Research is privileged to
be co-ordinating this Project. We are particularly grateful to The
Better Hong Kong Foundation whose support and assistance has
made it possible for us to conduct the present study, the results of
which are published in this monograph. The unfailing support of
many distinguished citizens in our endeavour and their words of
encouragement are especially gratifying. We also thank the
directors and editors of the City University of Hong Kong Press and
The Commercial Press (H.K.) Ltd. for their enthusiasm and
dedication which extends far beyond the call of duty.

Yue-Chim Richard Wong
Director
The Hong Kong Centre
for Economic Research

Foreword by the Series Editor

The population of Hong Kong has been ageing since the 1970s. According to official demographic statistics, those who were 65 and above accounted for 3.95% of the total population in 1967. By 1997, this ratio had risen to 10.37%. For the same period, the median population age increased over 70%, from 20.3 to 34.9.

The ageing of the population has been mainly the result of low birth rates and lengthened life expectancy. Since both of these factors will continue to exist in the foreseeable future, the ageing trend is expected to persist for some time.

To Hong Kong, an important economic implication of an ageing population is the rapid rise of the need for protection of the elderly after retirement. Traditionally, such protection comes from savings over the working years as well as support by children and relatives. The family has been a main form of resource allocation across generations.

Nevertheless, there are bound to be people with only limited productivity during work years, or those who have made wrong economic judgements when young, so that their savings are not sufficient to allow them to live decently through their retirement years. At the same time, the decline of the family in modern times makes it less reliable as a means of safeguard against shortfalls in old age. Retirement protection has thus become a significant part of government economic and social policy, especially for an ageing society.

In Hong Kong, discussion about government policies over retirement protection has spanned a lengthy period of about 30 years. It was only until recently that the decision has been made to institute the Mandatory Provident Fund (MPF). In other economies, various schemes of retirement protection have been practised over the past decades, with all kinds of experience that Hong Kong could beneficially refer to.

From a cash-flow point of view, retirement funds can be either "pay-as-you-go" or "fully-funded". From an operational point of view, they can either be managed by the government or the private sector. What are the pros and cons of these different kinds of schemes? Which one would be most appropriate for Hong Kong? As the details of the MPF have yet to be finalized, are there issues that are still worth attention and discussion?

This book analyzes all these questions in an organized and detailed manner. The author, Professor Francis Lui, discusses systematically the three major kinds of retirement protection: the "pay-as-you-go" system, the central provident fund, and the private pension funds. He substantiates his arguments by going through the historical developments of these schemes in other countries. Due coverage is given to the experience of the United States, China, Singapore, and Chile, among others. He concludes that private pension funds are superior to the other two schemes. Further, he makes specific proposals regarding the actual management of the MPF in Hong Kong.

Retirement protection is closely related to the issues of individual savings and investment on one hand, and social welfare on the other. It affects the economic well-being of all members of society, and, as Professor Lui notes, the performance of the economy as a whole. It is well worth the attention of everybody concerned. Professor Lui has undertaken research on this topic for a long time and he has published many papers on it. This book is a comprehensive representation of his views and findings, and is therefore a necessary reference for discussion on retirement protection in Hong Kong.

Y. F. Luk
School of Economics and Finance
The University of Hong Kong

Preface

I am indebted to many people who have helped me formulate the ideas contained in this book. Ten years ago I began my collaboration with Isaac Ehrlich on endogenous growth and social security. I have benefited greatly from the long hours engaged in stimulating discussion with him. Some of the material discussed in the book are outgrowths of our joint work. Colleagues at the Hong Kong University of Science and Technology and other tertiary institutions in Hong Kong have encouraged me to spend a great deal of time thinking about retirement-protection issues. Without their comments I would not have been able to develop many of the ideas presented in this book.

My students have always been an important source of stimulation. Their questions and comments helped me eliminate numerous nonessential elements from the manuscript. My research assistants, Chan Suk-ching and Cherry Tong, were instrumental in collecting materials and doing some of the calculations for the book. Pamela Tan of the Mandatory Provident Fund Office and Nelson Chow of The University of Hong Kong gave me valuable information. A referee provided constructive and thoughtful comments on an earlier draft. I am thankful for his/her criticisms. Richard Wong and Yim-fai Luk urged me to finish writing as early as possible. Without their encouragement this book would not have appeared.

Lastly, I am indebted to Francis Tsui for translating the manuscript into Chinese. A long-time friend and respected professional in mass media, Dr. Tsui is one of the few people whose translation I trust.

Francis T. Lui
Center for Economic Development
The Hong Kong University of
Science and Technology
December 1998

List of Illustrations

Figures

Tables

Acronyms and Abbreviations

Retirement Protection:
A Plan for Hong Kong

CHAPTER 1

Introduction: A Short History of the Debate over Retirement Protection in Hong Kong

After more than thirty years spent debating the costs and benefits of various retirement-protection options, the Hong Kong Government has finally chosen the Mandatory Provident Fund (MPF) as the main retirement-protection vehicle. The MPF is now official. In 1995 the Legislative Council (Legco) passed the primary legislation of the *Mandatory Provident Fund Schemes Ordinance*, and in 1998 the Provisional Legislature approved the remaining subsidiary legislation.

The main objective of this book is to examine and analyze the most important retirement-protection options that Hong Kong has considered. By adopting a consistent economic approach, I present theoretical arguments and empirical evidence to show that some of the politically popular options are either unsustainable or unnecessarily costly. Unlike some of the other options considered, the MPF is a nearly optimal system. Despite some of its limitations, it can serve as the foundation for building a robust retirement-protection system. In the book I discuss some key features of the newly adopted MPF, point out some of its weaknesses, and propose some ways in which it could be improved.

The book's secondary objective is to help readers understand the rationale behind the choice made by the legislature. Hong Kong was actually in an advantageous position when it made its decision.

Various forms of retirement protection had been in existence in different parts of the world for a long time. Enough information was available to allow us to assess the performance of these systems. Until the recent decision was made, Hong Kong had no formal retirement-protection system in place and was therefore free of any historical baggage that might have affected its objectivity. There was no need to incur any costs in "transiting" from an old system to a new one. The press in Hong Kong had been open minded about, and supportive of, the long and rigorous debates over retirement which are engaged in by the best-informed and most educated sector of the population. The central arguments of the debates, which are summarized in subsequent chapters of this book, touch upon many aspects of the theory and empirical literature of retirement protection. The book therefore provides a comprehensive review of the issues. It is my hope that this in itself is a contribution to the existing literature.

The book not only studies the substantive arguments for or against different retirement plans but also presents the fascinating history of the debate. The many events that occurred before the MPF was formally adopted can provide us with insight into the problems associated with the Hong Kong's transition into 1997. In this sense the book can be regarded as a case study of the social, economic, and political aspects of transition.

Events in Chronological Order

In this section I discuss the history of the debate over retirement protection in Hong Kong. I generally follow the chronological order of events related to the debate.

Legco first identified the retirement-protection problem as a matter worthy of its consideration in 1966. In that year, and once again in 1975, it debated whether a Singaporean type of Central Provident Fund (CPF) should be created in Hong Kong. The government also studied the viability of the system but decided not to pursue it.[1]

In 1987 a proposal made earlier to set up a CPF once again picked up momentum. On 13 May of that year, during a recess session of Legco, the issue was extensively debated. It did not receive enough support from Legco members, however; also, the government continued to oppose it. The main reasons given for this opposition were that the compulsory nature of the system would have many negative effects and that the system would not provide sufficient protection for the retired.[2]

Hong Kong waited four more years before the CPF was put on the Legco agenda again. On 10 July 1991 the Honourable Tam Yiu-Chung moved a motion to urge the government "to take immediate steps to re-examine the setting up of a Central Provident Fund or other forms of compulsory retirement schemes in order that workers in Hong Kong are provided with comprehensive retirement protection."[3] During the debate a member opined that a privatized pension system would be superior to a CPF. There were twenty-nine votes against the motion and eleven for it.

The 1991 motion seemed like just another futile attempt to set up a retirement system in Hong Kong. However, soon afterwards some concrete actions began to take place. In November 1991 the government took the initiative to form the "Working Group on Retirement Protection" headed by Mr. John Chan, the secretary of education and manpower. In October 1992, after almost a year of study, the working group came up with a consultation paper entitled "A Community-wide Retirement Protection System." The document proposed the establishment in Hong Kong of a compulsory pension system that, essentially, everyone would have to join. The proposed system would have been quite similar to the Chilean type of private pension system, which we shall discuss extensively in Chapter 4. However, it is not clear whether the working group was influenced by the Chilean system when it was crafting the proposal, because no mention was made of this system either in the document or in public discussions. As usual, the government spent several months soliciting opinions on the consultation paper. Before the consultation ended on 31 January

1993 the government had already made it clear that it would not consider the CPF as an alternative retirement-protection option.[4]

Politicians in Hong Kong did not seem fully satisfied with the government proposal. Some of them did not trust a plan in which the government had no central role. They picked investment risks and fraud as the line of attack and urged the government to act as the final guarantor. That this would be desirable was not agreed upon by everyone, however. Some pointed out that the guarantee could induce investors to act carelessly and aggressively.[5] However, criticism of the government gained momentum. On 3 February 1993 the Honourable Hui Yin-fat moved a motion on the CPF. An amendment made by the Honourable Tik Chi-yuen was successfully passed in Legco. The amendment urged the government to seriously consider the request made by members of the council to "expedite the establishment of a central provident fund scheme" (Hong Kong Legislative Council, 3 February 1993). The result was significant because it was the first time that enough support for the CPF had been mobilized in Legco. This was largely due to the change in position of a group of business politicians led by the Honourable Henry Tang.

Although the Legco vote did not have binding power, it put the government in a difficult position. The government continued to maintain its stand against the CPF, but it promised to reconsider the system (*Ming Pao*, 12 July 1993). After the end of the consultation period public debate in the press continued.

Mr. W. K. Lam, the acting secretary of education and manpower, was the chief government official in charge of the retirement issue during this period. His many public statements made it clear that the government was very much against the CPF even though it had promised to reconsider the plan. The private provident-fund scheme described in the 1992 consultation document was still the government's working proposal. There was also no indication that the government would support a pay-as-you-go (PAYG) type of retirement system, the features of which are discussed in detail in Chapter 2. In fact, as recently as November 1993 the acting secretary was still telling reporters that such a plan would not be suitable for Hong Kong.

It was therefore a big surprise to the public when Mr. W. K. Lam announced in Legco on 15 December 1993 that the government would give up the private pension plan and intended to adopt a PAYG welfare scheme, which was named the "Old-Age Pension Scheme" (OPS). Two important articles appearing in the *Hong Kong Economic Journal* on 12 January 1994 provide valuable information on the background of the change (see Fan, 1994, and Li, 1994). The "authoritative" tone of the articles and the inside information they reveal make it obvious that they were engineered by the government itself (see Chow, 1994). The articles admit that the public was very suspicious of the abrupt change. They try hard to provide justifications for the new government position. The article by Fan (1994) also details the chronology of some events.

The Executive Council of Hong Kong (Exco) heatedly debated the new proposal on 14 December 1993, one day before the announcement of the new proposal to Legco. In fact, Exco members themselves were surprised to learn about the new plan, which was unveiled only three days before they had to make a decision to support the plan. During the debate the OPS proposal was closely questioned by members with business backgrounds, but they seemed unable to come up with strong arguments against the plan. The proposal also had supporters, notable among whom was economist Edward Chen. Eventually it passed in Exco, with only one person, Tung Chee-Hwa, voting against it.

The OPS proposal initiated a flood of debate. Hundreds of articles and reports appeared in the print.[6] Numerous public forums on the subject were organized by various institutions. Many political parties, think tanks, and professional organizations issued position papers and reports on retirement systems. The government also took an active role and maintained an extraordinarily high profile in advertising the idea. With the help of a consulting company it hired, the government issued on 12 July 1994 a paper, "Taking the Worry Out of Growing Old," to justify its proposal.

The paper's consultation period lasted from July 1994 to the end of October 1994. Two sides seem to have gradually emerged out of the controversy. One side, led by the government and supported by some social workers, was for the OPS. The other side, whose arguments were articulated by economists and professional commentators in the media, was against the OPS and supportive of the privatized pension scheme.

The government proposal probably suffered its most severe blow when seventy-eight scholars, most of them academic economists, signed an open letter and published it in the form of a newspaper advertisement to oppose the OPS. In the open letter appearing in some major newspapers on 1 September 1994 and in the press conference held one day earlier, they articulated their opposition to the OPS and made three proposals, which are as follows:

1. Separate retirement protection and welfare for the aged.
2. The government establishes a CPF and implements a compulsory retirement protection scheme through legislation. Employees can freely choose to participate in either private pension schemes or the CPF. Pensions should be linked to contributions.
3. Old-age welfare is to be financed by government's revenue from general taxation. More cash subsidies and better medical, recreational, and housing service, etc. are to be provided to those elderly who are actually in need (*Hong Kong Economists*, 1994).

The economists' action apparently caught the government by surprise. Never before in Hong Kong's history had a large group of academics come together to issue a strong policy statement. Moreover, this group appeared to enjoy a high degree of prestige in Hong Kong. Their statement was extensively covered by the media, which generally showed a very positive attitude towards their position.[7] It should be fair to say that after their open petition was printed the press was tilted against the government proposal. Some proposals subsequently issued by political parties and think tanks also seemed strongly influenced by the academics' statement.[8] In November Legco even passed an amendment moved by the Honourable James Tien criticizing the OPS.

In the meantime the government continued to hard sell the OPS. It also spent money on TV commercials to advertise the system. The Acting Secretary of Education and Manpower was easily the most diligent government official willing to talk to the media and in public forums. China's official agencies occasionally voiced their concerns about the OPS. Very few people noticed that the pendulum was about to swing back to the other side.

In January 1995 the government surprised the public once again. It suddenly announced that it would abandon the OPS. The main reason given for this abandonment was that public opinion was too divided on the plan. To support this argument, the government published in January the analyses of public opinion on the OPS consultation paper (Hong Kong Government, Education and Manpower Branch 1995). According to the report, views among the 6,665 written submissions on the consultation paper were generally divided, with an even split between the number of supporters and opponents. The government also indicated that it would consider the private pension plan again.

On 8 March 1995 the government formally moved the following motion in Legco: "That this Council urges Government to introduce as expeditiously as possible a mandatory, privately managed occupational retirement protection system with provision for the preservation and portability of benefits" (Hong Kong Legislative Council 1995). According to the government there was no clear mandate to proceed with the OPS, but "there appeared to be broad acceptance of a mandatory, privately managed provident fund system (MPF)" (Willis 1995). As usual, the government made great efforts to lobby Legco members to vote for the motion. It also tried to lobby academics to support the new decision. The motion passed in Legco. The government was badly in need of this mandate to proceed with the building of a credible retirement plan.

At about the same time the government hired a different consulting company to perform a study on the feasibility of the

MPF. The company's report came out in April 1995 (Hewitt and GML, 1995). It provided some details to support the plan and made some specific recommendations. However, the spirit of the proposed scheme was similar to that described in John Chan's 1992 consultation paper. The government set up an MPF Office and appointed Pamela Tan to be the director. The office was responsible for working out the detailed design of the MPF and for writing it down in the form of legislation.

The government's frequent changes in direction aroused some suspicion among Hong Kong's citizens. Thoughts of a conspiracy theory were often in the back of some people's minds during a tense period for the Sino-British relationship. In May 1995 a mid-level official in the New China News Agency voiced his scepticism about the MPF. This announcement gave rise to some controversy in Hong Kong society. Governor Chris Patten complained that the agency had been against the OPS and that it was not right for it to oppose the MPF as well (*Hong Kong Commercial Daily*, 11 May 1995). Apparently, the official's remarks were his personal opinion. The New China News Agency did not offer any serious rebuttal at this time.

The government's strategy was to move quickly to pass the MPF legislation. To do this it adopted a two-stage approach. It first proposed the basic elements of the scheme and tried to get these passed in Legco. This could be done relatively rapidly and would give the government a sense of certainty that the approval of a retirement plan was feasible. In fact, the primary legislation, which was embodied in the MPF Schemes Ordinance, passed in Legco on 27 July 1995. With the enactment of the ordinance by the acting governor on 3 August 1995 the government proceeded to the second stage of its approach to pass the MPF legislation. This stage entailed the drawing up of subsidiary legislation before the MPF was put into practice.[9]

Supposedly, the subsidiary legislation was meant to embody the many details that would make the MPF operational and credible. The MPF Office probably anticipated that the completion of the subsidiary legislation could be done before the handover of Hong Kong to China took place on 1 July 1997. However, political reality made this impossible. There was a problem haunting the office and the entire legislative process. In the beginning, the government had not asked for enough funding to support the operation of the MPF Office. When existing money was about to be exhausted, the government had to request approval from Legco for additional funding. This gave politicians the golden opportunity to force the government to incorporate some of their proposals into the MPF. A long negotiation process between politicians and the government took place. It remains unclear whether some of the features of the MPF in place today are the result of rational thinking or of political bargaining.

Though the MPF Office was not able to complete the legislative process before the handover, this did not appear to present a major problem. The Provisional Legislature, which lasted from 1997 to 1998, was supportive of the scheme. The chief executive of the Hong Kong Special Administrative Region Government, Mr. Tung Chee-Hwa, also endorsed the MPF. The subsidiary legislation was passed in the Provisional Legislative Council on 1 April 1998. Two days later the council also approved funding for the establishment of the MPF Authority and the Compensation Fund. This should be regarded as a landmark in the history of retirement protection in Hong Kong. Although controversies will continue to appear, and although the MPF may be modified, the basic framework for retirement protection is in place.

Some Interpretations

We have just seen the tortuous process in developing a retirement-protection scheme for Hong Kong before the MPF was finally adopted. From 1966 to 1991 the government refused to consider the CPF or any other public scheme. Then in 1992 it proposed the establishment of a mandatory privatized pension plan. A year later it suddenly abandoned the proposal and tried to hard sell a scheme based on the other extreme, the PAYG OPS. In a matter of thirteen months the government changed its position again. It went back to the old proposal of establishing the MPF.

This sequence of events raises some interesting questions. The first question is, what were the reasons behind the changes in the government's position? Second, was the choice of the MPF as the retirement-protection plan for Hong Kong an inevitable outcome, or was it merely a historical coincidence?

It seems relatively easy to explain the government's reluctance to adopt a public retirement scheme prior to the 1990s. For several decades Hong Kong has adhered to the principle of so-called positive noninterventionism as its official economic policy. Government officials, for good or bad reasons, have been sceptical about putting the government in the position of managing a large sum of money. It is therefore quite natural that they did not like the idea of a Central Provident Fund.

The year 1991 was an important political milestone for Hong Kong. For the first time many members of Legco were democratically elected. It had become much more difficult for the government to maintain an executive-led system of policy making. The establishment of the Working Group and the proposal of a privatized system of retirement protection could be interpreted as preemptive moves against interventionist proposals that would be forthcoming from the more populist Legco.

Another plausible explanation for the proposal of a privatized retirement-protection system is that the government feared that the projected increase in welfare payments to the aged might impose a heavy burden on the government budget. According to a recent government-sponsored survey, the main source of income for more than three quarters of the old people in Hong Kong has been from their children. Moreover, the gross domestic saving rate in Hong Kong has been over 30% throughout the 1990s (World Bank, 1997a). Given such a high saving rate, we should expect most old people to be able to rely at least partially on their own savings during retirement. The increasing popularity of retiring in China, which is a much cheaper place, has made self-financing easier to manage. Despite the fact that the majority of the people in Hong Kong have not been relying on the government for retirement, we have to recognize that the population has been ageing rapidly.[10] The absolute number of people who will apply for old-age welfare support must go up in the future. By 1991 the government should have been well aware of this problem. It might have believed that the time had come to pay serious attention to the building of a formal retirement-protection system.

The private system gained little support in Legco in 1993. That year, some Legco members, usually regarded as representing business interests, claimed that the CPF would be appropriate for Hong Kong. Why did they change their long-standing position of opposition to the CPF? In retrospect, it is doubtful that they ever truly supported the CPF. By 1994 they had more or less ceased to make remarks supportive of it. They knew that the government would not adopt such a system. Supporting something that could not materialize would not threaten their interests and would also help them create an image of being concerned about the welfare of the elderly.

That the government moved in favour of the populist OPS is even more puzzling. The officials in charge should have known that adoption of the OPS would contradict what they had been preaching before the end of 1993. As has been pointed out by many commentators (e.g., Shum, 1994), only the governor, Chris Patten, had the authority to make such a decision to adopt the OPS. What could be the motive behind Patten's decision? As is discussed in Chapter 2, an advantage of the OPS is that it will benefit the old people of today. The costs, no matter how great, will only be paid in the future. As Hong Kong's last governor, by endorsing the system Patten might have been able to reap political gain, and he might have felt that the long-term benefits of Hong Kong society were not his problem, since he would no longer be associated with the city once the problems began having an effect. In light of this possibility, it is no wonder that Chinese officials in charge of Hong Kong matters were very suspicious of the OPS proposal.

Why did the government abandon the OPS eventually? If their motive for supporting it originally was political, the change would be understandable. As pointed out in the preceding section, even according to government assessment, public opinion on the OPS was divided. By the end of 1994 it was apparent that there was strong societal opposition to the OPS. That significant political gain could arise when supporting the OPS became less likely. Patten's incentive for going against the noninterventionist tradition of the economic bureaucrats had become much weaker. With historical hindsight, it is not really surprising that the government took up the cause of the MPF again.

Were the changes inevitable? To some extent they were. The government officials' free-market tradition was the basis of their opposition to a government-run CPF and OPS. On the other hand, the process of democratization in Hong Kong had prompted many politicians to side with such populist proposals. Society was also divided. The deterministic nature of events only applies up to this point, however. With divided views on the proposals, what the final decision would be was highly uncertain. Accidental factors could have played an important role here. The aforementioned petition signed by seventy-eight economists was apparently the turning point in the debate. Their ability to articulate the implications of the OPS gave rise to a great deal of public scepticism about the proposal. It appeared that Patten had not expected this development to occur. It is not unlikely that the OPS would have been adopted if there had been no such petition. As a person who watched this apolitical group's petition come into being, the author of this book believes that it was a purely accidental event. Some unplanned casual discussions among a small group of economists eventually led to their initiation of the petition.

Outline of the Book

This book has six chapters. Chapters 2 to 4 are devoted to discussing the advantages and disadvantages of the three main options for retirement protection, namely, the PAYG system, the CPF, and the privatized pension system. Theoretical considerations and different countries' experiences are presented. Chapter 5 examines Hong

Kong's situation and shows why the OPS is not suitable for the city. It also shows that the MPF can lay the foundation for a robust retirement-protection system. Some details of the MPF proposed by the government are also critically reviewed. Chapter 6 concludes.

Notes

1. The record of the debates in the Legislative Council provide a great deal of information on the issue. See for example, Hong Kong Legislative Council (10 July 1991), p. 98 and p. 124.

2. See the speech by the secretary of education and manpower in the Hong Kong Legislative Council, op. cit., p. 124.

3. Hong Kong Legislative Council, op. cit., p. 81.

4. See a report in *Ming Pao*, 12 July 1993.

5. For example, see Loh (1993).

6. For example, see Becker and Ehrlich (1994), and the articles collected in Lui (1995).

7. There were many reports and commentaries on the advertisement. For example, an editorial in the *South China Morning Post* on 2 September 1994 criticized the government's reaction to the academics' opinions. Chan (1994) said that the OPS suffered a major setback when it was condemned by seventy-eight economists. Shum (1994) urged the government to listen to the academics.

8. For example, see Liberal Party (1994) and One-Country-Two-Systems Economic Research Centre (1995).

9. See the letter from Cheung Chor-yung (1995), who wrote it in the capacity of an official in the Education and Manpower Branch.

10. Chapter 5 presents more detailed figures for the ageing problem.

11. After the OPS proposal was announced, some senior officials had to voice their endorsement. For example, the secretary of the treasury, Donald Tsang, said to the press at the time that this was a good plan. On 25 July 1997, in his keynote speech delivered at the Far Eastern Meetings of the Econometric Society, he severely criticized the OPS. It is doubtful that he had ever truly supported it. A knowledgeable government official told me in a private conversation in 1998 that the decision, which was opposed by officials in the Economic Services Branch, indeed came from Patten. The latter directed the officials to find reasons to justify it.

CHAPTER 2

The Pay-As-You-Go
Social Security System:
Theory and Practice

Among the different mandatory retirement-protection systems in the world, the pay-as-you-go (PAYG) type is the most common. Almost all industrial nations have established some variants of it. The social security systems in China and countries of the former Soviet Bloc also bear the main features of PAYG. Why is this system so pervasive? What are its theoretical implications? Can we draw some lessons from the experience of countries that have adopted it? These are some of the questions we must answer before we can come up with an optimal retirement-protection plan for Hong Kong.

This chapter contains two sections. The first section describes the most important elements of the PAYG system. Its advantages and disadvantages are also discussed. The second section is a review of several countries' experience with the system. This review serves two purposes. First, some of the hypotheses outlined in the first section can be tested. Second, it helps us identify some of the problems associated with the system. Application of the results of this chapter to Hong Kong's situation will be postponed until Chapter 5.

The Pros and Cons of the Pay-As-You-Go System

In this section I first describe the essential features of the PAYG system. Although in practice details of the systems in different countries may vary considerably, they must share some common features discussed below. When these are explained, some criteria for evaluating the system can be formulated. In particular, I discuss its pros and cons from six perspectives: (1) political attractiveness, (2) rate of return, (3) stability and sustainability, (4) fairness, (5) effects on savings, economic growth and fertility, and (6) risks involved.

The PAYG scheme, in its simplest form, is essentially welfare payments to the elderly financed by taxation. The government imposes a mandatory tax on the income — usually the wage income — of the working population.[1] The proceeds are not saved but are rather used immediately for pension payments; hence the term "pay-as-you-go".

There can be many deviations from this prototype. Sometimes the scheme's revenues may exceed its expenditures. The surpluses can form a fund that can be invested and used for future financing of payments. Typically, such a fund is not an integral part of the system, which should be distinguished from other fully funded saving schemes. The method used to calculate the pension for an individual may also differ among countries. At one extreme the pension is completely independent of previous tax payments. Alternatively, it can be indexed to wages.

A common feature of PAYG systems is that the employer is responsible for paying a portion of the social security tax on behalf of the employee. This should not be considered a reduction in the employee's tax rate. If a profit-maximizing employer has to pay, say, a 5% payroll tax for an employee, given enough time he will adjust the employee's salary downward by 5% to compensate for the loss. In the long run, it makes little difference who is paying for the payroll tax.

I now turn to the analysis of the advantages and disadvantages of the PAYG system. In so doing, I must establish some criteria for the evaluation. It is also necessary to understand whether there are hidden costs to the seemingly advantageous effects of the system. In short, we need to compare its costs and benefits.

Political Attractiveness

An important advantage of the PAYG system, it is often argued, is that once it is established the aged people of today can benefit from it immediately. These people did not pay any PAYG taxes, but they can receive pension benefits now. They are therefore net gainers. For people who are younger, determining the costs and benefits are more complicated. Unlike people who have already retired, they must pay the taxes. However, if they believe that the system is sustainable and that they are sure to get what they have been promised, they may be willing to interpret the tax payments as periodic contributions to an investment. Those who are close to retirement will not have to pay the taxes for long but can still anticipate full retirement benefits. They may also gain from the system. Young people and the working population will have to pay the taxes for a long time. They may gain or lose, depending on how much they have to pay and how much they can get back in the end.

From politicians' point of view the PAYG system is attractive. First, there seems to be a sizeable portion of the population that can benefit from the scheme. Politicians may be able to get some popular support by advocating it. Second, when there are losers, they are likely to be the youngest cohort of the population. If the losers are in the minority, politicians can ignore them. The youngest cohorts may also lose because they cannot shorten the tax-payment period. However, they are not voters yet. Myopic politicians can brush them aside.

There are limits to the above arguments. It is conceivable that some older people, knowing that their children must bear the tax burden, may oppose the scheme. This fact by itself is already cause for apprehension if parents care about the welfare of their children. Moreover, knowing that the government will provide pensions, young working adults may reduce the amount of their support for their parents. Thus, even elderly people do not necessarily gain from the system.

Most PAYG schemes contain an income-redistribution compo-nent. The most obvious example of this component is that, under the scheme, everybody is guaranteed some uniform monthly payments irrespective of how much tax they have paid. In some schemes social security benefits are not completely detached from previous tax payments, but the links are weak. Poor people are more likely to support these schemes, whereas the middle class may oppose them. Thus age and income are two of the relevant factors determining an individual's political support of the PAYG system.

Rate of Return

Although the taxes paid for a PAYG scheme are not meant to be saved for future uses, people may still look at the system as an investment vehicle. The present discounted values of the tax payments and pension benefits can be compared to determine whether people are better off as a result of the scheme. One convenient way to make this comparison is to treat taxes as an investment and to compute the rate of return. The higher are the latter, the better is the scheme.

Population structure and the rate of growth of the wage rate are the two most important factors that determine the rate of return of participation in the scheme. The reason for this is simple. After paying taxes during the working years, how much can a retired person expect to get back? This depends on how much tax revenue will flow into the system. If the support ratio, or the number of persons of working age for each person of retirement age, increases, then more people can pay taxes. Alternatively, total tax revenue can increase faster when the average wage rate has a higher rate of growth. Both of these effects will raise an average person's pension benefits. Obviously, the opposite is true if the population is ageing very rapidly and while the wage rate is stagnant or even declining.

A simple example will serve to illustrate this point. Imagine that people in every generation only live for two periods of equal length, the young period and the old period. In other words, society is always inhabited by overlapping generations of otherwise identical young and old people. People work and pay equal amount of taxes when young, retire and receive pension benefits when old. Assume that the population is increasing over time such that the number of people in a new generation is always twice that of the old generation. Also, suppose that the wage rate doubles in every period. If the tax rate remains constant, then for every dollar paid when young, a person can expect to get back four dollars when old. This is because there will be twice as many taxpayers, each of them paying twice as much as members of the older generation did.

In practice, the length of the retirement period may not be the same as the working period. People's wages and pension benefits may differ across individuals. The growth rates of their wages may also vary. Nevertheless, the main idea in the above illustration remains viable. An increase in the support ratio, or faster growth of the average wage rate, will raise the rate of return of a PAYG scheme for people belonging to every income class.

The above discussion implies that the PAYG option is better suited to a society whose population is getting younger, that is, one in which the support ratio is increasing over time. People will also gain more if the wage rate is going up faster. However, these conditions do not apply in most developed countries, the populations of which are ageing quickly. People not only live longer but also have fewer children. The total fertility rate, that is, the number of children that an average woman expects to bear in her lifetime, typically remains below two.[2] This implies that the number of people in a new generation is declining relative to the number in the old generation. If the wage rate is also stagnant, and if the tax rate does not change, then the rates of return of the PAYG schemes in these countries could be negative.

When there is an income redistributive component built into the scheme, the rates of return for people of different income classes will differ. It is possible that poorer people can still enjoy a positive rate of return, whereas richer groups suffer losses. Nevertheless, the faster is the population ageing process and the slower is the growth of the wage rate, the greater the proportion of people losing under the PAYG scheme will be. Thus, under these circumstances, it is reasonable to ask whether there are alternative schemes that will make everybody better off.

Stability and Sustainability

As discussed above, a property of the PAYG scheme often regarded as its main advantage is that in the initial phase elderly people can benefit without their having had to pay any social security taxes in the past. Where does this free lunch come from? Upon closer examination, there are indeed hidden costs behind the scheme. The lunch is not free.

A simple way to identify the hidden costs is to find out what will happen if the system is terminated. In the initial stage of the scheme, as mentioned above, elderly people are eligible to receive pension benefits without paying the costs. However, after several decades, as the system matures, the beneficiaries should have all paid taxes in the past. Obviously these taxpayers all stand to lose once the PAYG scheme comes to an end. Some people can gain at the inception of the system only because future generations have to bear the potential losses. In other words the system imposes monetary transfers from future to current generations. Those living in the future will not necessarily lose if the system can last forever. But can it really be sustained perpetually?

To answer this question, it is useful to note that the PAYG system shares some important properties of the so-called Ponzi, or pyramid, scheme.[3] The main elements of the Ponzi scheme, which is named after its inventor, an Italian who emigrated to the United States in the early part of the twentieth century, can be described as follows.

Imagine that a fund manager announces an "investment" plan for people to participate in. The manager guarantees an extraordinarily high rate of return. However, after people have deposited money into the fund, it is not invested. If some people decide to withdraw, the fund manager lives up to his or her promise to return the money, plus the accrued interest, to the participant. Given that there is no investment, what is the source of the interest income? When it is generally believed that the rate of return is high enough, many customers will be attracted to "invest" in the plan. So long as the inflow of funds exceeds the outflow, the scheme is viable. Over time, the size of the fund can actually become very large if this pattern continues. However, once people begin to cast doubt on the scheme, or the outflow begins to exceed the inflow, the scheme is doomed to collapse. The fund manager may grab the entire remaining sum and disappear.[4]

The PAYG system resembles the Ponzi scheme in several ways. First, taxes collected for the PAYG system are not invested. The same is true for funds deposited in a Ponzi scheme. Second, people eligible to receive social security benefits during the early stage of the system may enjoy a high rate of return. At a later stage, if the system runs into difficulty or comes to an end, people who have paid the taxes will have to suffer losses. Similarly, participants in a Ponzi scheme can benefit only if they are able to withdraw money before it breaks down. Third, as long as the incoming social security taxes exceed or equal the outgoing payments, the PAYG system will suffer no immediate crisis. A Ponzi scheme does not necessarily collapse if the inflow of money is bigger than the outflow.

Earlier I argued that the implicit rate of return from participating in a PAYG scheme depends on the population structure and on the growth rate of the wages. In most developed countries there is significant ageing of the population. Moreover, possibly because of easier access to new supplies of cheap labour from some developing countries and the former centrally planned economies (like China and countries in Eastern Europe), the real wage rates in many developed countries have been stagnant or have even been declining.[5] Both of these factors imply that the PAYG system cannot yield any high returns and possibly may even yield significantly negative returns for participants. This will create great political difficulties for the government. In principle, the government can deal with the problem in two different ways.

The first is to maintain a reasonably high rate of return for the system. Given the decline in the support ratio and in real wages, the government must increase the tax rate so as to balance the budget. However, raising the tax rate today implies that workers of the current generation have to pay more for the scheme. In the future, when they retire, they will expect more benefits. This will exert greater pressure to further increase the tax rate. In fact, as we shall see in the next section of this chapter, most countries seem to be experiencing an upward trend in the social security tax rate. However, the tax rate cannot be increased indefinitely, because doing so will result in conflicts with taxpayers. Raising the tax rate does not mean that participants in the PAYG scheme will not have to suffer losses. It only postpones these losses. The cost of doing so is that the liabilities of the scheme will grow bigger and bigger. They could be likened to a time bomb threatening the stability of the economy.

The second approach is to ignore the problems caused by the low or negative rate of return and focus on balancing the budget. In order to cut costs the government can lower the pension benefits or postpone the retirement age. The latter in effect amounts to forcing people to lengthen their tax-paying period and to reducing the time span for receiving benefits. Taxpayers are happier if the government takes this approach. If the first approach is used, retired people will suffer losses. They will invariably resent the reduction of benefits.

Neither of these approaches can really resolve the difficulty the government has to face, nor can a combination of the two approaches. In an environment where the population is ageing and the wage rate stagnant, it is not possible to maintain a reasonably high rate of return and a low tax rate simultaneously without causing a long-term budgetary crisis. Whether the system is sustainable becomes questionable. However, once the scheme is in place, it is extremely difficult to abolish. Since there is no easy way to compensate those who have paid the taxes for their losses, the problem may continue to drag on, becoming more and more difficult to resolve.

Fairness

At the inception of a PAYG system the government is imposing some intergenerational transfers from our descendants to the old people of today. Raising the social security tax would start a chain of effects. More wealth is transferred from the young to the old.

Because today's young people have paid more taxes, they will ask for more benefits in the future. They will pressure the government to further increase the tax rate when they retire. That will again initiate another series of transfers from future to current generations. Are there compelling reasons based on fairness to justify these transfers?

One argument is that the old tend to be poorer and that therefore society's income distribution is made more equal by such transfers. A study by the World Bank (1994, p. 11) casts serious doubt on this claim, however. In most countries the young, especially those with small children in their families, are on average poorer than the old. This is partly because the richer groups tend to live longer, whereas those with low incomes are more likely to die at a younger age.

Even if our goal is to redistribute income from the rich to the poor, to do so through the PAYG scheme is not efficient. Its pension payments are not means tested. This implies that young families with low incomes have to subsidize old people who may be wealthy. This problem could be exacerbated because, as mentioned above, rich people tend to live longer and therefore will receive more pension payments than the poor do. Welfare payments based on a means test appear to be a fairer and more effective instrument for income redistribution.

Another argument is that the elderly have already contributed to society's development and therefore have the right to receive pension payments from the government. There are problems with this rhetoric, however. Although it is not disputed that many retired individuals did contribute significantly to society during their younger days, they were already fully compensated for these contributions by their salaries. If they are eligible for pension payments now, in the final analysis, it is not the government but rather taxpayers of the younger generations who are actually providing the support. The latter may readily accept their responsibility to help their own parents. They may not, on the other hand, necessarily agree that they are obliged to support old people from other families.

A budgetary crisis, we should not forget, can in principle lead to the reduction of benefits or even to the abolition of the system.[6] When this occurs those who have paid the taxes will lose. Which generation will stand to lose depends on when the budgetary crisis takes place. It is hard to justify the view that the direction of inter-generational transfers should depend on the timing of the crisis. On the grounds of fairness, it seems that a better redistributive scheme should be neutral with respect to generations. The PAYG system is not fair in this respect.

Effects on Saving, Economic Growth, Fertility and Labour Supply

The PAYG system involves tax payments. It is well known that most taxes create distortions in the market. It should hardly surprise us to find that similar effects are attributable to the scheme. This subsection discusses several possible sources of distortions.

The issue of whether a PAYG system has any negative effects on saving is a matter of considerable controversy. The matter is important because it is often believed that a declining saving rate may hurt the level of income in society.[7] Feldstein (1974) argues that the scheme reduces the economy's saving rate. When taxes are collected they are not saved. A taxpayer expects that pensions will be paid to him in the future. Hence, he can reduce his savings earmarked for retirement. Total savings in society will thus decline.[8] Barro (1974, 1978) and his followers, who advocate the concept of Ricardian Equivalence, have seriously challenged this view. Parents who are altruistic towards their children understand that the social security benefits they are going to receive will have to be financed by taxes imposed on their children. At equilibrium, the present discounted values of the benefits and the taxes are equal. As a result, parents do not believe that their families are getting any net welfare benefits from the system. Their behaviour in terms of saving does not change.

On the empirical side, the issue of whether PAYG social security has adverse effect on savings has been extensively tested.[9] The studies have come up with different conclusions, depending on the particular data set and model used. It may be premature to pass a negative judgement on the PAYG scheme on the ground that it lowers the saving rate in the economy. We need to look at other criteria as well. A relevant question to ask is that of whether the system will lower the long-term economic growth rate. The answer is important because, as Lucas (1988) has rightly demonstrated, a small reduction in the long-term growth can result in huge losses aggregated over time.

Various authors have pointed out the possibility that the PAYG system may lower the long-term growth rate of the economy (see e.g., World Bank, 1994). Ehrlich and Lui (1997) demonstrate theoretically that the system may indeed reduce the growth rate in developed countries but that its effects in less-developed countries are uncertain. In a society without any social security system, care and material support from the children constitute important contributions towards the livelihood of the elderly. Hence, the number of children and their education level (and their income) are decisive factors determining benefits that people can enjoy during their retirement years. On the other hand, under a PAYG system, since financial support depends on taxes collected by the government, benefits are independent of the number of one's children and on their income level. Therefore, under such a system there are incentives for the citizens to act as free riders. They depend entirely on their government and "eat from the big rice bowl". Consequently, investment in their children will become less important.

In developing countries the social security system may create incentives for parents to limit the size of their families, which may be good for economic growth. In high-income countries where birth rates are already at very low levels, however, the main effect of the social security system is to reduce investment in the education of children. This, in turn, will have negative effects on the economic growth rate. There is no doubt that parents care for their children and invest in their education, despite the existence of a social security system. The point is that some parents would naturally do less of it because of the system.[10]

These hypotheses have been tested with 1960 to 1985 data from a relatively large sample of countries. The results confirm what has been discussed above. In particular, social security tax as a percentage of the GDP has a significant and adverse effect on the long-term growth rate in developed countries. In poorer countries, however, it is the fertility rate that is depressed by the PAYG scheme. One may note that in the literature the negative effect on fertility has been used extensively as a test for the existence and importance of the old-age support motive for having children.[11]

In Corsetti and Schmidt-Hebbel (1997), an endogenous growth model is constructed to examine the possible effects of changing a PAYG to a fully funded system. The real-world example that the authors try to model is that of Chile. Using simulation exercises they have obtained results showing that the PAYG system reduces economic growth.

In Chapter 5, I argue that the PAYG system's negative effect on the growth rate is one of the reasons that it is not a good system for Hong Kong. Based on the quantitative estimate of the magnitude of the effect, one can calculate the total foregone losses that could occur if this system were established. The losses could be huge.

One of the common criticisms levied against a welfare system is that it creates distortions in the labour market. The PAYG scheme, which has the characteristics of a welfare system, is also the target of such criticism. Because, in most cases, retirement benefits are not linked to tax payments, people have less incentive to work when the PAYG tax-rate goes up. This in turn adversely affects the GDP of an economy. However, the importance of this effect should not be overstated. Though it is true that the level of the GDP may go down as a result of the adoption of a PAYG system, there is little reason to believe that labour-market distortions of this type can lower the economy's long-run growth rate.

Risks

Some people believe that the PAYG scheme has the advantage of being the safest retirement system. If old parents depend primarily on their children for support, they may be subject to the risks of default or of their children dying. On the other hand, when saving is the basic means for retirement protection, people have to face investment-fraud risks and the ups and downs of the market. This view exaggerates the stability of the PAYG system, however, and ignores methods available to reduce the risks associated with other retirement-protection options.

In less developed countries where the mortality rate is high, parents often choose to bear more children. One interpretation of this choice is that it can reduce the risk of a child's death affecting the livelihood of his or her elderly parents in the later years of their life. The likelihood that no child will take on the responsibility of supporting his or her parents is also lower when there are more children. Default risks can be decreased further by educating (or indoctrinating, depending on the way one views it) children as to the importance of filial piety. Peer pressure is often used effectively in this regard. Investment risks cannot be avoided entirely, but diversifying the investment portfolio can significantly reduce such risks. It should also be noted that retirement funds are usually long-term investments. Short-term volatility does not have much of an effect on long-term performance.

As the World Bank (1994, p. 11) report has correctly pointed out, the view that only governments can insure against group risks is a myth. In fact, the PAYG system is subject to considerable political, income, and demographic risks. Most governments do not index PAYG pension benefits for inflation. This allows them to escape budgetary difficulties. However, pensioners do not know when political or budgetary considerations will lead the government to redefine the benefits, as it often does. Moreover, under the PAYG system the value of pension depends on how much tax can be collected, which in turn depends on the prevailing average wage rate. The latter is a variable that is subject to considerable fluctuations in the labour market. Demographic changes are another source of uncertainty for the PAYG system. As discussed earlier in this chapter, the ageing of the population will definitely affect the financial viability of the scheme. It should also be added that geographical mobility of labour will affect tax

Table 2.1
Financial Characteristics of PAYG Pension Schemes
in Transition Economies, 1992
(%)

	Pension Expenditures as a Share of GDP	Employee Contribution Rate as a Share of Net Wage	Employee-employer Contribution Rate as a Share of Net Wage
Hungary	10.6*	35	53
Poland	11.4	30	43
Romania	6.7	16.5–25.9	31–41
Czechoslovakia	9.5*	30	50
Bulgaria	8.4	26.7–38	35–50
Albania	6.3	25	26
Slovenia	13.0	30	41
Russia	4.9	32	40

Source: Fox (1994, p. 4).

Note: * 1991 figures.

revenues, and hence benefits, as well. It is not true that the PAYG system involves very little risk or that other methods involve more uncertainties.

Several Countries' Experiences

In the last section of this chapter, I will discuss several criteria by which to assess the pros and cons of the PAYG system. From the theoretical point of view the disadvantages seem to outweigh the advantages, even though the system is politically attractive. It remains for us to examine the actual experience of this system in different countries.

An implication of the PAYG system is that when it matures, either the tax rate rises to a very high level or the government has to figure out some way to cut the benefits. Eastern Europe's experience clearly demonstrates that the PAYG tax rate can get unacceptably high. In Table 2.1 the employee-employer combined contribution rate as a share of net wage ranges from 26% to as much as 53% (last column). Pension expenditure as a share of GDP can also be as high as 13%. In OECD countries the situation seems to be better.

However, employees in these countries have also accumulated large PAYG entitlements that the governments will eventually have to pay back. Pension debt, that is, the present value of the entitlements, varies from 90% of GDP in the United States to nearly 240% in Italy (van der Noord and Herd, 1993). National debts of OECD countries usually triple once we include net pension debts. And sometimes the size of the pension debt and the financial health of the system are not all that matter. In Japan the estimated (net) pension debt in 1990 was 137% of the GDP in that year.[12] But a perhaps even more severe problem facing Japan is that its excess fiscal burden caused by social security is unevenly distributed across generations (Hatta et al., 1997).

Some countries have tried to overcome the PAYG system's tendency to cause tax rates to steadily increase by cutting benefits or shortening the period during which retirees are eligible to collect benefits. Examples of such attempts are numerous. Before 1992 Italy's retirement ages for men and women, respectively, were sixty and fifty-five. In the year 2003 that age for men will be raised to sixty-five, and by the year 2012 the age for women will go up to sixty-five (Campbell, 1992). Similarly, in 1993 Sweden reduced pensions to 98% of exiting benefit levels. It also raised the retirement age from sixty-five to sixty-six over a period of four years (Kritzer, 1993). We should realize that the decrease in lifetime benefits is equivalent to a reduction in the implicit rate of return of the PAYG system.

These events are far from unique. If we study the different countries case by case we can see the ideas outlined in Section 1 emerging again and again. In the interest of conserving space I will only discuss in detail the experience of three countries: Germany, the United States, and China.

Germany [13]

In 1889 Bismarck put into place in Germany the world's first mandatory PAYG pension system. Before that time various retirement plans had existed. As early as the Middle Ages miners established provident funds to cover different kinds of risks (Steinmeyer 1991, pp. 75–76). Eventually miners' participation in such programmes became compulsory. In 1825 Prussian civil servants also established a mandatory pension scheme. The use of this type of scheme gradually spread. By the 1860s about half of the industrial workers and miners had joined some insurance programmes mandated by government for economic protection.

Bismarck's main motive for introducing the PAYG programme was political. He was competing with his adversaries, the Social Democrats, and this measure, which some socialists advocated, could be used to undermine the support of the Social Democrats by the working class (Schulz et al., 1974, p. 5). Originally Bismarck wanted to establish a noncontributory scheme so that the state would build a benevolent image. The middle class, which believed in self-sufficiency, opposed it. The scheme that was actually put into place required contributions from workers and had few redistributive effects. Moreover, it only provided for benefits at the subsistence level.

The first old-age pensions, involving about 600,000 beneficiaries, were paid in 1899. They were not available to people under the age of seventy. Since the vast majority of German workers died before this age, most people received no benefits.

In 1911 a new programme was introduced. White collar workers had to contribute more, but they were also entitled to more benefits. More significant changes occurred in 1957 when the Pension Reform Act was introduced. At that time benefits increased substantially. The legislation also called for future annual indexation of pension benefits. In practice this was based on changes in wage levels. In 1972 the pension policy was revised further. Some people retiring at the age of sixty-three were allowed full pension benefits without having to pay any penalty. Moreover, those who had paid the PAYG taxes for more than twenty-five years were given the option of choosing a minimum benefit package equal to 75% of the average wage of the period. This was a major step towards building an element of income redistribution into the pension scheme, although under the scheme benefits were still collected largely in relation to earnings.

The pension scheme's expanding benefits, along with demographic changes, inevitably increased the tax burden. When the system was first introduced in the nineteenth century the scheme's combined tax rate, collected from the employee and from the employer, was 1.7% of the wage, but by 1989 it had risen to 18.7% (International Benefit Guidelines 1989, p. 95). Pension payment as a share of GDP also reached 11.8% in 1985 (OECD 1988).

As the tax rate increased there was pressure to reform the system. This pressure was reinforced by demographic projections indicating that the number of pensioners per person in the labour force would go from today's (1990s) 0.5 to 1 by the year 2030 (Williamson and Pampel 1993, p. 33). People were very fearful that the financial viability of the system would break down if this trend continued. In 1989 new legislation was passed to make the indexing procedure less generous. The annual adjustment rate for pension benefits was reduced.

The German experience with the PAYG system is important because it was the first country in which the system was used. What does Germany's story tell us? Its PAYG system began modestly because tax and benefit levels were very low. However, there was no guarantee that they would remain low perpetually. Political pressure gradually mounted, and benefits increased. Germany's experience with this aspect of the system fails to support a claim made by the Hong Kong Government about its own yet-to-be introduced PAYG system in 1994. In that year, in order to win political support for its newly proposed PAYG scheme, the government argued that the contribution rate was low and would remain so because people would not agree to increase it in the future (Lui 1995, chapters 27 and 28). Changes in Hong Kong's demographic structure, and in particular, the ageing of the population, strongly suggest that the tax rate under the PAYG scheme would have increased, just as it did in Germany. Fears of a budgetary crisis lying ahead might force the government to reduce benefit levels. This would lower the rate of return for people who had been paying taxes at a high rate. The German experience does not present an exception to the difficulties inherent in a PAYG system outlined in the first section of this chapter.

The United States

The American experience with the PAYG system in many ways resembles that of Germany. In 1934 President Roosevelt formed the Committee on Economic Security to draft the Social Security Act. In 1935 the act was formally enacted by the federal government, even though many states had already established old-age pension schemes of their own during an earlier period. The pensions in the 1935 act were compulsory, contributory, and earnings related but were not means tested. However, about 40% of the labour force was excluded from the scheme. Tax payments into the scheme began in 1935, but the law specified that pensions would only start in 1942 and would be paid to people over the age of sixty-five (Williamson and Pampel 1993). Thus the system was not exactly a PAYG scheme in the beginning. Roosevelt hoped that the reserves accumulated in the trust fund between 1935 and 1942 would make the system self-supporting and not dependent on federal revenues (Schulz 1988, p. 124).

Subsequent developments of the scheme did not fully follow Roosevelt's intentions. As early as 1939, before the scheduled date of the first pension payments had arrived, the programme had already been modified. Influenced by the Keynesians, the economic doctrine prevalent at the time dictated that funds should not accumulate in the hands of the government. Instead the funds should be spent to stimulate the economy. It was decided that the first pension payments would be made in 1940, two years earlier than the original plan had indicated. Benefits were also extended to the wife and children of the covered worker, whether he was alive or deceased. The money accumulated in previous years in part prompted this change. The system was changing from a nearly fully funded scheme to one that was PAYG. The trust fund in effect became a kind of contingency reserve (Williamson and Pampel 1993).

Benefit levels were raised in subsequent years. In 1950 they increased by 77% so as to restore their purchasing power to 1940 levels (Kingston 1987, p. 25). In 1956 disability insurance was added, and in 1965 hospital insurance for the elderly was included. Indexation of pensions began in 1972. In that year the Supplemental Security Income (SSI) programme was enacted, which also allowed some people who had not paid any PAYG taxes to become eligible for benefits.

The first serious but short-term financial difficulty of the programme occurred in 1977, when the economy was weak. At that time the Social Security Act was amended to replace the old indexing formula by a cost-of-living-adjustment (COLA) formula. This lowered the actual amount of benefit payments. More changes involving reduction of benefits took place under the Reagan administration. Survivor benefits to students aged between eighteen and twenty-one were dropped in 1981. The most important amendments occurred in 1983, when social security pensions ceased to be tax exempt. In that year it was also decided that the age of eligibility for full pension benefits would gradually increase from sixty-five to sixty-seven between the years 2000 and 2027. COLA would be based on increases in prices or wages, whichever was lower.

We can see from the above historical outline of the American retirement-protection system that net benefits increased in the beginning but were reduced later on. On the other hand, the tax rate had been going up monotonically. As is evidenced by Table 2.2, the combined social security tax rate (which was shared equally by the employer and employee) in 1937 was 2% of earnings. By 1990 it had gone up to 15.3%. It should be noted that a portion of taxes is earmarked for disability and medical insurance. However, the pension component, or Old-Age Security Insurance (OASI) had also reached 11.2% (5.6% x 2) of earnings in 1990.

Will the reduction in U.S. social security benefits effected by the 1983 amendment and the rising PAYG tax rate resolve the budgetary problem permanently? The intention of the so-called Greenspan Commission, which prepared the 1983 amendment, was to create a trust fund using the surpluses amassed as a result of

Table 2.2
PAYG Tax Rates in the United States, 1937–97

| Year | Tax Rate (%) Employer and Employee, Each | |
	Total	Old-Aged Security Insurance
1937	1.0	1.0
1950	1.5	1.5
1954	2.0	2.0
1957	2.25	2.0
1959	2.5	2.25
1960	3.0	2.75
1962	3.125	2.875
1963	3.625	3.375
1966	4.2	3.5
1967	4.4	3.55
1968	4.4	3.325
1969	4.8	3.725
1970	4.8	3.65
1971	5.2	4.05
1973	5.85	4.3
1974	5.85	4.375
1978	6.05	4.275
1979	6.13	4.33
1980	6.13	4.52
1981	6.65	4.7
1982	6.7	4.575
1983	6.7	4.775
1984	7.0	5.2
1985	7.05	5.2
1986	7.15	5.2
1988	7.51	5.53
1990	7.65	5.6
1997	7.65	5.6

Source: *Social Security Bulletin*, Annual Statistical Supplement, various years.

the increasing tax rate and of declining benefits. The fund had to be large enough to offset the predictably huge increase in PAYG taxes of the children of baby boomers. However, less than one and a half decades after the amendment passed, many people have come to believe that the original assessment of the social security budget situation was far too optimistic. Some have projected that the trust fund will be used up as early as 2029. The social security tax will have to increase to 20% of earnings in order to avoid this situation.

Since Medicare tax is expected to go up to about 10% of earnings, the total tax rate on today's kids, not including income tax, will have to be almost 30% in the United States' future (Kotlikoff 1996).

These projections and the fear that the ageing of the baby boomers will create a budgetary crisis prompted a large group of American economists to endorse a proposal for reform written by two prominent economists, Laurence Kotlikoff and Jeffrey Sachs (1997). The main thrust of the proposal was that a personalized fully funded system should be introduced to replace the PAYG system. During the transition period, social security retirement benefits would be financed by a new federal retail-sales tax.

The U.S. Government was also concerned about the possible budgetary crisis. A thirteen-member Advisory Council on Social Security was formed to study the problem. As is stated in its report, "all council members agree that the pay-as-you-go approach should be changed" (Advisory Council on Social Security, 1997). Members have also recommended investing more of the trust fund in stocks, whose expected yield is higher than is that of bonds. However, they are split regarding the method of reforming the PAYG system.

What conclusions can we draw from the history of the PAYG system in the United States? We see clearly the rising trend in the tax rate. In the beginning many people did benefit from the system. However, this was at the expense of intergenerational inequity. Later generations had to pay high taxes and to face the possibility of reduced benefits. Although the extent of the recent budgetary crisis has been subject to a controversial debate, any possible remedy, given the large number of ageing baby boomers, will mean either cutting benefits or increasing the tax rate even further. Again, the American experience is supportive of the points raised in the first section of this chapter.

China

As Table 2.3 shows, more than two-thirds of the old people in China rely primarily on kinship support during their retirement. China's officially instituted pension system is a variant of the PAYG

Table 2.3

**Percentage of Chinese Population Aged Sixty-Five
and Above by Their Major Source of Income, 1994**

Income from Work	Retirement Pension	Income from Premium and Relief	Income from Kinship	Others
15.93%	14.08%	1.58%	67.39%	1.02%

Source: Based on the 0.63% sample population survey conducted in China on 1
          October 1994. See *China Statistical Yearbook* (1995), p. 66, Table 3.9.

type, but only 14% of the elderly citizens depend on it as their major
source of income. Even though this proportion is relatively small,
China's experience with it offers valuable lessons in a number of
respects. First, it clearly demonstrates that retirement protection is
not a free lunch but can be very costly if the system is not
appropriate. Second, the difficulties caused by the demographic
structure are similar to those Germany and the United States have
had to deal with. They emerge irrespective of whatever type of
culture or society we are considering. Third, China's reform of the
retirement system may provide useful information on how to phase
out a PAYG scheme, if its attempt to do so proves successful.

In 1951 the Interim Labour Insurance Regulations specified
two sets of regulations governing the retirement benefits of employees in China's state-owned enterprises and civil service. These
employees did not have to contribute to a pension plan. Expenditures were ultimately guaranteed by the government irrespective of
the financial solvency of the enterprises. Retirement pay was at least
60% of a worker's wages, based on the last month of salary
received. All the administrative work of the social security system
was performed by the individual's work unit. Benefits were not
portable. These programmes are still operating today.

Since 1978 a number of changes to the system have been
effected. Pension payments were adjusted a number of times to cope
with inflation. The mandatory retirement age was enforced at sixty
for men and fifty-five for women. People of poor health could retire
ten years earlier. The continuous-service requirement, which was

an eligibility condition for benefits, was shortened to ten years. Local governments were allowed to carry out various experiments on social security (Liu 1991). As a result, some cities and provinces came up with programmes substantially different from the norm set by the central government (Liu 1993). It was not uncommon for retirement benefits to exceed 90% of the wage rate (Liu 1991). Not surprisingly, both the number of beneficiaries and the benefit levels measured in various ways increased significantly.

The increase in expenditures inevitably imposed a great financial burden on work units, especially state-owned enterprises. Many of them became uncompetitive. This was more serious when the proportion of old people in a particular enterprise was higher than usual. When the government tried to pool the retirement systems of different enterprises together so as to reduce risks, many enterprises with a lot of young workers refused to participate. To pay for the losses of the state-owned enterprises, the central government often had to resort to printing more money. An almost perpetual high-inflation problem in China was largely caused by this practice (Lui 1995, chapter 14). Inflation reduces the purchasing power of people's monetary assets. So it is like a tax that is imposed on them. Thus, benefits for the old are created by the transfer of wealth from the young to the old through the inflationary policy.

The system caused two long term problems for society. First, labour mobility was reduced because people were afraid that their benefits would not be portable. Second, although life expectancy in China was less than seventy years in 1994 (World Bank 1996b), its population is expected to age rapidly. Table 2.4 shows that in less than fifty years its support ratio will drop from the current 10.6 to 3.3. If China is already experiencing financial difficulties now, the burden will only be more severe in the future. A group of experts at the World Bank have estimated that by 2033, if the PAYG system is not reformed, it will require a contribution rate of 39%. The system is simply not sustainable (World Bank 1996a, 1997b).

On the more optimistic side, as the World Bank has argued, reforming China's system will probably not be that costly (World

Chapter 2

Table 2.4
Changes in Population Age Structure in China

Age	1994	2000	2005	2010	2020	2030	2040
15–64 (%)	66.6	66.6	68.6	70.9	70.2	67.6	64.3
65+ (%)	6.3	6.3	7.3	7.8	10.9	14.5	19.5
Support Ratio	10.6	10.6	9.4	9.1	6.4	4.7	3.3

Sources: The Figures for 1994 are adapted from the 0.63 sample population survey conducted on 1 October 1994. See *China Statistical Yearbook* (1995). Post-1994 projections are from Lin and Lu (1994, p. 43). Support ratio is equal to the proportion of people aged fifteen to sixty-four divided by the proportion of people aged sixty-five and above.

Bank 1996a, 1997b). Life expectancy in China is not yet as high as it is in other industrialized countries. The support ratio is still over 10. There may still be enough time to carry out a reform. The current benefit levels, which exceed international standards, could be reduced. We can also recall from Table 2.3 that the proportion of old people relying on pensions in China is relatively low. The World Bank's detailed calculations indicate that the transition to a system with a Chilean-type provident fund is feasible.

To conclude, all the examples discussed here demonstrate that there are inherent difficulties that plague the PAYG system. Many countries that have adopted it must now consider ways to move towards a fully funded system, which, as we shall see in the next two chapters, are immune to the problems suffered by the PAYG. In designing a retirement system for Hong Kong we must consider the issues carefully and take care not to repeat the mistakes that other countries have made with the PAYG system.

Notes

1. Sometimes, for political expedience, advocates of the system may label tax payments as "contributions". For example, in 1994, when the Hong Kong Government proposed a PAYG scheme, it refused to admit that the payments were taxes on the ground that the proceeds were set aside for a special purpose. See Lui (1995, chapter 26) for more details. Such

payments are surely taxes. They are mandatory, and there is no legal guarantee that the government will repay them upon an individual's retirement.

2. See the statistics on life expectancy and total fertility rate in the World Bank (1996a).

3. Samuelson (1975) is one of the first papers to recognize that the PAYG system resembles a Ponzi scheme. Also see Lui (1995, chapter 28) and Disney (1996, p. 307).

4. For an example of such malpractice in Hong Kong in 1994 see Lui (1995, chapter 28). Indeed Ponzi himself was prosecuted for creating the plan. See Russell (1973).

5. Examples of declining real wage rates can be found easily. Government statistics indicate that for a long time the growth rate of the real wage rate in Hong Kong has been below the growth rate of per capita real GDP. In the manufacturing sector real wages have been declining during the last several years. See Hong Kong Government, *Hong Kong Monthly Digest of Statistics*, various issues. The real wage rate in the United States has also been declining for a long time. Between 1980 and 1995 it decreased by 5%. See United States Government, *Statistical Abstracts of the United States*, 1996, p. 424.

6. As I discuss in Chapter 4, Chile is an example of a country in which the PAYG system is close to being abolished.

7. In neoclassical growth models, the steady-state economic growth rate is not affected by the saving rate. However, in the short term, the reduction in capital accumulation caused by the decline in saving can still lower the level of income.

8. Feldstein's argument is meant for the PAYG system only. In 1991 it was used mistakenly by legislator Stephen Cheong in the Legco debate on the CPF. See minutes of the Hong Kong Legislative Council, 10 July 1991, pp. 84–85.

9. For example, see Feldstein (1974, 1980, 1995), Munnell (1974), Esposito (1978), Kotlikoff (1979), and Leimer and Lesnoy (1982).

10. The discussion here follows that in Lui (1991).

11. For example, see Entwisle and Winegarden (1984), Nugent (1985), Nugent and Gillaspy (1983). Also see Ehrlich and Lui (1997) for a review of the literature on old-age support motive.

12. If the pension system is partially funded rather than purely PAYG, it is better to use the concept, "net pension debt." It is the balance between the accumulated pension fund and the pension debt. If the system is fully

funded, the net pension debt is zero. In the case of a PAYG system, the pension debt is the same as the net pension debt.

13. For a detailed discussion of the development of pension systems in Germany, see Williamson and Pampel (1993).

CHAPTER 3

The Central
Provident Fund

General Aspects of the Central Provident Fund

The CPF is one of the most important retirement-protection options that Hong Kong has considered. Some countries have been using the system for long period of time, and enough experience has been accumulated for us to form a judgment of this system. In fact, it has been debated in Hong Kong's Legco several times since the 1960s, the most recent debate having taken place in 1993. Since a Legco voting in February of that year urged the government to consider the system seriously, it had become a topic of extensive controversy in Hong Kong society. Even today there are still powerful political lobby groups that want to set it up in Hong Kong.[1] The Hong Kong Government has never agreed to establish it, however.

The theoretical implications of a CPF are much simpler than those of the PAYG system. What are the CPF main features? There are three. First, the CPF is a forced-saving system. People must contribute a specified portion of their income to a fund earmarked for providing pensions. Second, the fund is managed centrally by the government. In some cases the government may delegate part of the management responsibility to private companies. Third, each person contributing to the fund has an individual account. He may or may not have the freedom to choose the investment options, but he has private property rights over the amount accumulated in his account. In other words, there is no income-redistribution component built into the system.

Table 3.1

Contribution Rates and Assets of Selected Central Provident Funds

Countries	Contribution Rate as Percentage of Wages (1991)			Asset of CPF as Percentage of GDP (most recent year available)
	Employee	Employer	Combined	
Singapore	22.5	17.5	40	75.6 (1991)
Malaysia	9	11	20	40.8 (1991)
Fiji	7	7	14	43.9 (1987)
India	10	10	20	4.5 (1990)
Indonesia	1	2	3	1.4 (1990)

Sources: Adapted from World Bank (1994), Tables 6.2 and 6.3. Contribution rates in Singapore are from Wong (1993).

One common question about the CPF is whether it can provide adequate support for retirement. The Mathematical Appendix at the end of this book provides a formula for calculating the monthly pension payment under a forced-saving retirement scheme. This formula is applicable both to the CPF and to the privately managed provident fund, which will be discussed in chapters 4 and 5. In general, the monthly payment available for retirement depends on a number of factors. Increases in the monthly income during the working period, the contribution rate, the real rates of return for the investment before and after retirement, the length of the working period, or the growth rate of the real wage rate will raise the absolute amount of the monthly pension payment. On the other hand, if the duration of the retirement period is longer, then the monthly pension will go down. It is evident that when retirement is postponed pension payments will be larger, because people have more time to save and less time to spend. As pointed out earlier, if the growth rate of the real wage is higher, pension payment will increase. However, pension payment as a portion of the wage rate just before retirement, or the so-called "replacement ratio," will decline when the wage rate increases fast. This is because a person's wage level before retirement will be much higher than his or her wage rate today. Thus, the answer to the question of whether there will be sufficient funds to cover pension payments depends entirely on the values of the parameters mentioned above.

The first CPF was established in Malaysia in 1951. Subsequently, Singapore, India, Indonesia, and some African, Caribbean, and Pacific countries followed Malaysia's lead. In several countries the system failed and was abolished. As can be seen from Table 3.1, both in terms of contribution rates and in terms of the value of the assets as a percentage of GDP, the CPF in Singapore is the most important and the largest. For this reason, I shall discuss it in greater detail after we discuss the issue of evaluating the CPF.

Evaluating the CPF

Like any issue that has remained controversial for a long time, the CPF has many explicit and subtle implications that are not well understood by society. To assess the usefulness of CPF as a retirement system we need to discuss those implications carefully. In this section, the advantages and disadvantages common to all CPFs are addressed.

The fundamental assumption used to justify the CPF, or any other form of forced-saving scheme, is that people are myopic and are incapable of financially planning for their retirement unless the government steps in. Some may argue that there are two advantages for the government to do so. First, there is a better guarantee that people will have greater security during their retirement years, because the amount they save will be larger. Second, a higher rate of saving means faster accumulation of capital, and this in turn raises the economic growth rate.[2] These advantages, even if they are real, may have been exaggerated, however.

Do people really save less for retirement in the absence of forced saving? If it is well understood that old people will have to support themselves, then a rational person, say a woman, must find ways to prepare for her retirement well ahead of time. After all, she has several decades to observe the consequences of ignoring it. Suppose she has chosen to save 30% of her income. Then the government establishes a rule requiring her to contribute 10% of her income to a CPF. Will she now save 40%? Probably not. Since 30% is the rate she has chosen, she must believe that this is the most suitable rate for her. To maintain this rate she will simply reduce her deposits to her private account and transfer them to the CPF. The total amount she saves does not change.

There are conditions under which the above scenario does not apply. An obvious case is one in which the mandatory saving rate of the CPF is higher than people's desired saving rate. They will then have no choice but to save more than what they would like. Another example involves means-tested welfare programmes aimed at supporting old people. If a person has already saved enough she may not pass the means test and will not be eligible for the welfare payments. In this case she may strategically choose a lower saving rate so as to increase the chance of being eligible for welfare payments. The resulting saving rate will then be too low to be socially optimal. A forced-saving scheme may help to prevent this from happening.

We should note that a person saves money for different reasons during her life. In the absence of a CPF, a young person probably saves because she wants to get married or to raise children. When she is older her saving are used for her children's education. She begins to save exclusively for retirement probably only when she is in her forties or fifties. The CPF forces her to begin saving for retirement earlier than she wants to. Her saving rate may indeed be raised by the CPF. However, when she gets older and sees that she has already accumulated some money in the CPF, she will decide to reduce her saving rate. Thus, the CPF alters the saving pattern over the course of a person's life but does not necessarily raise the average saving rate in a society that is inhabited by people of different ages. The CPF is likely to increase the national saving rate of a society dominated by a young population. However, the rate will decline when people in this age group get older.

Two statements can summarize the above discussion. First, immediately after the introduction of the CPF, or any other form of forced saving, to a society, the society's saving rate will go up. Second, after two or three decades, it is possible that the saving rate will drop back to the old level, provided that the forced-saving rate is not higher than the voluntary saving rate. Fund managers who are eager to exploit the opportunities offered by a forced-saving scheme are often overly optimistic about the long-run positive effect on the saving rate.

Because available empirical data are limited, it is difficult to estimate the effect of the CPF on the national saving rate. However, the case of Hong Kong does provide an example indicating that the saving rate can be very high even though a forced saving scheme does not exist. Hong Kong's gross domestic saving rate in 1995 was 32%, which was among the highest in the world.[3] It is true that Singapore's rate is an astonishing 51% (World Bank, 1996b). However, it would be a big surprise if the Singaporean rate were not higher than the socially optimal level.

In addition to the positive effect on saving, the CPF has other properties that are often interpreted as advantages. Some believe that the administrative expenses of the CPF are on average lower than are those of privately managed funds. A number of arguments can justify this belief. First, the government is not a profit-making enterprise and therefore charges lower fees for its services. Second, the government is big enough to take advantage of economies of scale to improve its efficiency. Third, it can free ride on its bureaucracy to facilitate collection of contributions and payments of benefits. While these arguments may very well be valid, it is difficult to assess their importance. Moreover, precisely because the government does not try to maximize profit, it is doubtful that it has as much of an incentive as a private fund does to minimize the costs of operation.

It is often argued that the CPF offers the advantage of portability. When an employee changes jobs there is no need for him to shift to another fund. With the new job, he can continue to inject new contributions into his old account. This property is indeed attractive because frequent movement from one fund to another increases the transaction costs involved. Nevertheless, as

Table 3.2

**Average Annual Real Returns for Selected Publicly
and Privately Managed Pension Funds, 1980s**

Management	Country	Period	Real Rate of Return
Public	Peru	1981–88	–37.4
Public	Turkey	1984–88	–23.8
Public	Zambia	1980–88	–23.4
Public	Venezuela	1980–89	–15.3
Public	Egypt	1981–89	–11.7
Public	Ecuador	1980–86	–10.0
Public	Kenya	1980–90	–3.8
Public	India	1980–90	0.3
Public	Singapore	1980–90	3.0
Public	Malaysia	1980–90	4.6
Public	United States (OASI)	1980–90	4.8
Private	Netherlands (occupational)	1980–90	6.7
Private	United States (occupational)	1980–90	8.0
Private	United Kingdom (occupational)	1980–90	8.8
Private	Chile (AFPs)	1981–90	12.3

Source: Adapted from World Bank (1994, p. 95). The rates of return are not adjusted
          for administrative costs. In the case of Chile's AFP, average net returns, after
          deducting the administrative expenses, is 9.2%. See Chapter 4 also.

will be argued in the next chapter, there is no inherent reason that a
system of privately managed funds cannot do the same thing.

Security is another advantage of the CPF that has been cited.
Many people believe that an institution run by the government is
financially more secure than one run by a private company. This
belief is justified because the government is backed by its almost
unlimited taxing power. One should not, however, forget that
governments can be overthrown. The degree of security of the funds
entrusted to the government depends on how stable the latter is.

An important property of the CPF distinguishes it from the
PAYG system. As demonstrated in the last chapter, the implicit rate
of return in the latter system depends critically on the demographic
structure of a society. If a population is aging, the rate of return is
pulled downwards. The CPF is immune to this drawback. Its rate of
return is independent of the proportion of old people to young
people because the amount in an individual's account is privately

owned. However, if the retirement period is longer, the CPF's monthly benefit level will obviously be lower.

A fundamental criticism of the CPF as a retirement-protection system is that there are inherent inefficiencies when market activities are replaced by government decisions. In the case of the CPF, there appear to be two main sources of inefficiencies. First, there is lack of competition when the government is the sole manager of the fund. This reduces the government's incentive to look for more profitable investment opportunities. Second, the main desire of CPF participants is to secure as large a sum as possible at retirement. This goal is not necessarily compatible with the agenda of government bureaucrats. The latter generally prefer a low-level risk for investment, although this may be at the expense of reducing the rate of return. They cannot gain much for themselves when the fund is performing well. On the other hand, when the fund is losing money, they will be subject to a lot of public pressure. Their optimal strategy is therefore to manage the investment in an overly conservative way. Moreover, to make the investment decisions of a CPF politically independent is not easy. Politicians and interest groups often find other people's money in the CPF a convenient instrument for achieving their own political objectives. They may lobby or pressure the government to spend the money on politically popular projects, such as building bridges and highways, even though the rates of return for such projects are worse than those for other projects. A CPF could mean that the allocation of a substantial amount of society's wealth is determined politically. It is hard to believe that the outcome will be efficient.

The suggestion that publicly managed funds do not yield high rates of return is consistent with empirical observations. In Table 3.2 the average rates of return for publicly managed funds are compared with those for privately managed funds. The contrast is clear. A large proportion of public funds have recorded negative real rates of return. Those that have achieved positive returns have been able to do so only at modest levels. On the other hand, the returns of private funds are impressive. Chile, for example, has a spectacular real return of 12.3% a year. After adjusting for the

Table 3.3
Ratio of Contribution to Singapore's CPF (in % of Wage Income)

Year	Employee	Employer	Total
1955	5.0	5.0	10.0
1961	5.0	5.0	10.0
1968	6.5	6.5	13.0
1969	6.5	6.5	13.0
1970	8.0	8.0	16.0
1971	10.0	10.0	20.0
1972	10.0	14.0	24.0
1973	11.0	15.0	26.0
1974	15.0	15.0	30.0
1975	15.0	15.0	30.0
1976	15.0	15.0	30.0
1977	15.5	15.5	31.0
1978	16.5	16.5	33.0
1979	16.5	20.5	37.0
1980	18.0	20.5	38.5
1981	22.0	20.5	42.5
1982	23.0	22.0	45.0
1983	23.0	23.0	46.0
1984	25.0	25.0	50.0
1985	25.0	25.0	50.0
1986	25.0	10.0	35.0
1987	25.0	10.0	36.0
1988	24.0	12.0	38.0
1989	23.0	15.0	38.0
1990	23.0	16.5	39.5
1991	22.5	17.5	40.0
1992	22.0	18.0	40.0
1996	20.0	20.0	40.0

Sources: Adopted from Tay (1992), Wong (1993), and Low (1996).

exceptionally high administrative costs incurred as a result of the start-up expenses of the system, the real rate of return is still at the high level of 9.2% for that period.[4] Thus available evidence suggests that private funds perform significantly better than public funds.

Another potential problem of the CPF is that when it is in place, a significant portion of society's wealth is under the control of the government. Even if we ignore the possibility of government failures, the scarcity of private funds may suffocate investments in the market. This in turn limits opportunities for the development of entrepreneurial spirit in society. To the extent that the latter often plays an important role in the income growth of a free market economy, the CPF may have a negative impact on people's income.

Some of the negative effects of a CPF system can be mitigated by a certain degree of decentralization. For example, the government may delegate the responsibility for managing the funds to some private investment houses. The latter have to compete by virtue of their performance in order to win larger shares of the funds. The government may also permit people to withdraw a portion of the funds in the CPF for private investment. The implications of this will be discussed in detail in Chapter 5.

Singapore's CPF

In this section we critically review Singapore's experience with its CPF. Such a review is useful because it tells us what a successful CPF can and cannot do. The evolution of Singapore's system also illustrates some of the CPF's inherent problems and suggests ways in which they can be resolved.

Singapore's CPF was established by the British Colonial Government in 1953 and became operative in 1955.[5] In the beginning it was a relatively simple forced-saving scheme. Employers and employees both contributed 5% of an employee's wages into the CPF. The contributions were tax exempted. People were not allowed to withdraw money from the CPF until they were fifty-five years of age. Since the adoption of the plan, however, several major changes have been made to it.

Table 3.3 shows the contribution rates in various years since the inception of the CPF. There was a general increasing trend from 1955 to 1984, when the combined rate reached 50% of the employee's wages. There have been some fluctuations since then, and the combined rate now is 40%. The reduction in 1986 was mainly a result of the 1985–86 recession. The Singaporean government lowered the employer's contribution rate to 10% in that year. It was thought at the time that this could help cut costs

Table 3.4
Nominal Interest Rates of the Singapore's CPF

From	Nominal Interest Rate
1961	2.50
1963	5.00
1964	5.25
1967	5.50
1970	5.75
1974	6.50
Mar. 1986	5.78
Jul. 1986	5.38
Jan. 1987	4.34
Jul. 1987	3.31
Jan. 1988	3.19
Jul. 1988	2.96
Jan. 1989	3.10
Jul. 1989	3.39
Jan. 1990	3.77
Jul. 1990	3.88
Jan. 1991	4.85
Jul. 1991	4.54
Jan. 1992	4.59

Source: Singapore, Central Provident Fund Board, Annual Report, various years.

and make the economy more competitive internationally (Tay 1992). However, it should be pointed out that in a fully competitive market it is immaterial whether the reduction in contributions to the fund comes about as a result of the employer's or the employee's contribution, or of the wage rate itself. What really matters is the total compensation package.

An important measure of the CPF's performance is its rate of return. The CPF's main source of income is interest payments from government bonds. Historically most of the deposits in the CPF were used to purchase government bonds. For example, in 1980, 95.1% of the fund was used to buy Singaporean government bonds. Today the proportion has increased to 100% (see Low 1996). From 1961 to February 1986 the nominal interest rate remained stable for prolonged periods because the CPF Board believed that it should be independent of the market rate. This policy was changed. Since March 1986 the rate has been adjusted periodically to reflect market conditions. In practice the board sets it equal to the simple average of month-end interest rate for one-year fixed deposits and savings accounts by four major Singapore banks (Tay 1992). The average nominal interest rate from 1961 to 1992 was 5.4%, whereas the real rate was only 2.1% (Wong 1993). The rate of return for investment in Singapore's CPF is modest.

Initially the CPF was solely a pension scheme, and participants could not withdraw money before they reached the age of fifty-five. However, over the years a process of liberalization has been underway.[6] The CPF has become a multipurpose scheme. In 1968 the legislation was amended to allow members to use their CPF savings before they reached the age of fifty-five to finance down payments and amortize loans for buying low-cost public flats. Since 1981 eligible people using CPF money to pay for loan instalments for public housing have been automatically placed under the Home Protection Insurance Scheme. In that year members of the CPF were also allowed to use CPF money to redeem all or part of their housing loans on their first private residential properties. This privilege was extended in 1986 to certain nonresidential properties such as office space, factories, and warehouses. As of 1988 the maximum amount that members were permitted to withdraw was 80% to 100% of the value of private properties.

The liberalization process also applies to other investment vehicles. Since 1986 the Approved Investment Scheme has enabled members to use their CPF savings to buy approved shares, convertible loan stocks, unit trusts, gold certificates, gold saving accounts, and physical gold. In the beginning the main restriction was that people were allowed to withdraw only 40% of their "investment savings", that is, savings that exceeded a certain minimum sum in their accounts. The minimum sum was adjusted periodically. In 1993 it was S$33,800. In the same year a new scheme was introduced. It allowed the use of up to 80% of investment savings. A second plan, the Enhanced Investment Scheme, was also introduced to broaden investment options for CPF members who had larger sums in the CPF. They could use part of the CPF money to invest in stocks and other securities. These two

Table 3.5

Withdrawals of CPF by Type (in millions of dollars)

	1985	1990	1995
Total	3,360 (100%)	3,995 (100%)	7,253 (100%)
Public Housing	1,785 (53.1%)	1,252 (31.3%)	2,782 (38.4%)
Residential Properties	782 (23.3%)	1,007 (25.2%)	1,809 (24.9%)
Reached Fifty-Five Years of Age	506 (15.1%)	803 (20.1%)	1,112 (15.3%)
Leaving Singapore and Malaysia Permanently	146 (4.3%)	156 (3.9%)	241 (3.3%)
Death	41 (1.2%)	54 (1.4%)	88 (1.2%)
Medisave Scheme	44 (1.3%)	208 (5.2%)	296 (4.1%)
Others	56 (1.7%)	515 (12.9%)	925 (12.8%)

Source: Singapore, Department of Statistics, Yearbook of Statistics, 1995.

plans were expected to free up a total of 17 billion Singaporean dollars for investment. These new plans were greeted jubilantly by the community as a late Chinese New Year present (Ng 1993).

The multifunctional nature of the CPF has also been evidenced by the establishment of the Medisave system in 1984. Under this scheme CPF members and their immediate family members can use their savings in the so-called Medisave Account within the CPF to pay for hospitalization expenses. Since 1986 they have been allowed to use it for outpatient charges as well. In case the amount in the Medisave is not sufficient, they can "borrow" from their expected future contributions.

The data shown in Table 3.5 make it difficult to argue that providing a retirement pension is the sole or even the main objective of the CPF. Of the total amount withdrawn from the fund in 1995 only 13.5% was for retirement. In fact, by 1995 the total due to members in the CPF had grown to S$66 billion (Singapore, *Yearbook of Statistics* 1995). The number of participants had also increased to 1.3 million. Given that so much wealth is controlled by the CPF and that providing elderly citizens with a pension is no longer its most important objective, it is reasonable to question why the system should continue to exist in its current form.

There are actually two issues involved. First, should such a large-scale compulsory saving scheme be run by the government?

Second, is the liberalization process justified? Regarding the first issue, we should note that almost the entire amount in the CPF has been lent to the government. Once this loan has been made the government has full control over the resources. This brings out the classical problem of whether the government is a good substitute for private individuals when decisions about resource allocation are to be made. From the point of view of social efficiency it is doubtful that the overall performance of the government is superior to that of a private individual. Actually, the very fact that people have been eager to withdraw their money from the CPF to invest it in other vehicles shows that they believe they can make use of the resources more efficiently than the government can. On the second issue, relaxing some of the restrictions on the withdrawal age means that the government is returning to the people part of the ownership control of their resources. Some of the negative effects of the CPF we discussed earlier in this chapter can indeed be mitigated. The popularity of the new changes is an indication that the government has pursued the right policy. However, in this case one must ask why the government should compel people to contribute so much in the first place.

The main justification for the high contribution rate seems to be a political one. In a revealing interview conducted in 1993, Senior Minister Lee Kuan Yew said:

> "Singapore has no choice. We must have a defence capability. That means man must have something to fight for. He is not going to fight for somebody else's Rolls-Royce or Mercedes 600. He's got to fight for what he or his family owns.
>
> "So we had to devise a system which gave everybody a home, which he owns. Everyone has something substantial in property. Everyone has a retirement account and medical cost account." (*South China Morning Post*, 27 November 1993).

Even if we agree that stakeholdership may improve loyalty and stability in Singapore, we may still question whether there may be

better ways to accomplish this objective than this paternalistic
approach. In particular, when people have improved control of
their wealth, they may also buy Singaporean assets if the returns are
high enough. Using the rate of return and the risks involved to guide
an investment is demonstrably a more efficient mechanism for
resource allocation. In principle more wealth can be created when
investments are efficient. In the long run the stake will be even more
valuable. In fact, some people believe that the CPF is best character-
ized as a hostage held firmly in the government's hands. When the
government controls so much private wealth it is less likely that
people will go against its wishes.

Notes

1. There were hundreds of newspaper reports and articles on the controversy surrounding the CPF in 1993. For example, see the report about
   pensions in the *South China Morning Post* on 14 December 1993, an editorial in the same newspaper on 15 December 1993, and articles on 7
   November 1993.

2. Strictly speaking, an increase in the saving rate can only raise the
   economy's short-run but not necessarily its long-run growth rate. This is
   because the marginal product of capital tends to decline when more and
   more capital has been accumulated. See Solow (1956) and the vast
   literature on endogenous growth.

3. See World Bank (1997a). Some countries that have the CPF have a lower
   saving rate than Hong Kong. For example, India's gross domestic saving
   rate in 1994 was 21%, and that in Indonesia was 30%.

4. See Chapter 4 for more details on the Chilean system.

5. For a brief review of the history of the CPF see also Low (1996).

6. See Tay (1992) and Low (1996) for more details on the liberalization.

CHAPTER 4

The Private Pension Systems of Chile and Other Countries

Private pension schemes have long been in existence. They are an important form of retirement protection in many countries, especially in those with well-developed financial sectors. In 1981 a series of events had led the Chilean government to introduce a new form of private pension. This time it was the government that promulgated laws to establish the schemes. However, unlike the CPF, these schemes were decentralized and privately administered. A number of countries have since then followed Chile's example to establish similar systems. In Chile's case there is an element of compulsion to join the scheme, but in other countries that have adopted such systems this is not necessarily the case.

In this chapter I review Chile's experience with its pension system. Such a review will be useful for any economy, Hong Kong included, that plans to set up a similar scheme. There are five sections in the chapter. In the following section I discuss the history of, and rationale for, the establishment of the Chilean private-pension scheme. In the second section the details of the scheme are outlined. An important problem that Chile had to resolve was how the existing PAYG system could be phased out. The third section discusses the policies relating to the transition to the new scheme. In the fourth section I address some of the problems and difficulties of such a retirement system, using Chile's experiences as illustrations. The fifth section shows how some countries have modified Chile's system to suit their own needs. The chapter concludes with some brief remarks.

Retirement Protection before 1981

Chile was the first country in the western hemisphere to establish a comprehensive PAYG social security system, which it put into place in 1924.[1] Strictly speaking, it was not a single system, but rather, more than thirty systems based on occupation. The most important three of these systems, which in 1979 enlisted 94% of the contributors, were for government employees, salaried employees, and manual workers. The contribution and indexation rates, benefit levels, and requirements for retirement of each were different. However, retirement age was the same for all of them.

Beginning in the 1970s a single method for benefits indexing was introduced in Chile. The retirement age was raised to sixty-five for men and to sixty for women. The government also began to limit the wage and pension adjustment to a level below the inflation rate. These modifications eased the budgetary burden of the PAYG system. However, they were far from sufficient to resolve its financial difficulties, especially those induced by the declining support ratio, that is, the ratio of active contributors to pensioners.[2] Because all workers were guaranteed a minimum pension, they and their employers had an incentive to avoid making contributions as much as possible. Moreover, many people tried to underreport their earnings up until the last five years of service, since these were the only years used for computing actual benefits. The economic crisis of the early 1970s raised the unemployment rate to three times its previous level. The government was forced to lower the social security contribution rate in order to stimulate employment. Apparently this did not help much. Tax evasion was still common. The support ratio had declined to 2.5 to 1 (Castillo 1993, p. 408). Social security deficit was as high as 25% of the GDP at that time. In 1981, when the economic situation had improved, the implicit overall debt of the PAYG system was still 80% of GDP (World Bank 1996a).

During the late 1970s it was clear that the PAYG system had to be reformed. The military government finally decided to switch to a totally new system. There was little opposition to abolishing the old system, because under that system 93% of the pensioners could receive only the minimum amount of benefits determined by the government. The new system to be introduced was the *Administradora de Fondos de Pensiones* (AFP; Privately Managed Pension Fund).

Institutional Details and Performance of the AFP

Chile's Legislative Decree No. 3500 of November 1980 established the AFP, which became operative in May of the following year. Wage earners were given five years, until 1986, to decide whether they should remain in the PAYG system or join an AFP. Participants in an AFP are required to pay 10% of their earnings into a privately managed pension fund. Coverage for old age is provided. If an employee wants to be eligible for the disability and survivors' benefits, an additional 2.5% to 3.7% of earnings must be contributed (International Labour office 1994). This has to be provided in its entirety by the employee. Neither the state nor the employers are required to contribute (Gillion and Bonilla 1992, p. 172). Managers of the AFP, after deducting a commission, invest the money on behalf of the participants. Each of the latter owns a separate account in the AFP. Pension benefits depend on the amount accumulated in his account plus interests accrued.[3] Money in the AFP is both portable and transparent. Workers can move freely from one AFP to another. They can check the current valuation of their account and the commission charges at any time.

The private-sector AFPs are regulated by the *Superintendencia de Administradoras de Fondos de Pensiones* (SAFP), which is a state organization.[4] It is empowered to approve or reject the creation of new AFPs, supervise their operations, ensure their compliance with legal requirements, suggest regulatory reforms, provide compulsory rules for applications by the AFPs, levy fines, and enforce the winding up of the AFPs. Each AFP must set up a limited company to administer the pension funds. Managers of the AFP must keep their own assets separate from the funds of members.

The SAFP also establishes investment rules that the AFPs must observe. These rules, however, are adjusted from time to time. Initially, investments were limited to state (treasury and central bank) liabilities, bank liabilities, and mortgage and corporate bonds. Upper bounds on their shares in the investment portfolio were imposed. Over time these upper bounds have been modified, and new investment instruments, including foreign securities, are now permitted (Vittas and Iglesias 1992). In October 1991 the portfolio of the AFPs was already well diversified: 38.47% was in treasury bonds, 25.31% was in financial institutions, 25.41% was in equities, 10.74% was in public and private bonds, and 0.07% was in cash (Gillion and Bonilla 1992).

According to current regulations, workers who have a reasonable history of contributions are guaranteed a minimum pension when they reach the age of sixty-five for men and sixty for women. In case a worker's accumulated fund in the AFP is not big enough for him to draw this minimum, the state will have to make up the difference. To prevent the state from being overburdened, AFPs are required to generate for each month a return that is at least as big as one of the following, whichever is lower: "(a) the average profitability over the previous 12 months of all the funds administered by the AFPs, minus 2 percentage points; or (b) 50 per cent of the average profitability over the previous 12 months of all such funds" (Gillion and Bonilla 1992).

To ensure this minimum monthly rate of return AFPs must establish a Fluctuating Profit Reserve and a Guarantee Reserve. The former consists of those profits in excess of one of the following, whichever is higher: (a) the average profits over the previous twelve months of all AFPs, plus two percentage points; or (b) such profits plus 50%. The latter is equal to 1% of members' accumulated funds, after deducting some exemptions, which include investments in short-term bonds issued by the General Treasury or the Central Bank of Chile and investments in other funds. If these reserves are not sufficient to guarantee the minimum rate of returns, the state will again make up the difference and punish the AFP by dissolving it (Gillion and Bonilla 1992).

Guarantees by the state often induce various forms of moral-hazard behaviour. The commitment by the state to making up the difference in case the pension funds fall short of the minimum level could increase the average degree of investment risks in the economy. Investors, knowing that the state will back them up when they lose money, are more willing to choose a higher-risk portfolio because it is expected to yield a better return rate. The Fluctuating Profit Reserve in the Chilean system appears to be an approach to dealing with this problem. We can look at it from the point of view of an AFP manager. Suppose that he invests in high-risk securities. He may be able to get high returns, but the excess profit has to be put into the reserve. Members of the AFP do not necessarily gain all the benefits from the high returns. On the other hand, the big risk he has taken may increase the likelihood that the fund will suffer losses. Under such condition the SAFP will wind up the fund. Thus, the AFP is not adequately rewarded for achieving high returns, but it is penalized for making high-risk investments. The incentive to engage in the type of moral-hazard behaviour discussed above is thereby weakened. This advantage of the Fluctuating Profit Reserve, however, does not come without cost. We shall see in the fourth section of this chapter that this reserve may be one of the reasons behind the high administrative expenses of the Chilean pension system.

The state's guarantee also creates another kind of moral hazard that cannot be corrected by the Fluctuating Profit Reserve. Low-income workers who have not saved enough in the AFP have an incentive to delay or evade payments when they are near retirement. Whether they continue to pay or not, they can still get the minimum pension provided by the government. Indeed, the compliance rates of contribution for AFPs targeted at low-income groups have experienced some declines (Gillion and Bonilla 1992). High-income workers are not subject to this type of moral hazard. Their pension benefits are linked to how much they have contributed.

Chapter 4

Table 4.1
Real Rate of Return for Chilean Pension Funds

Year	Rate of Return (%)
1981	12.5
1982	26.8
1983	22.7
1984	2.8
1985	13.4
1986	12.0
1987	6.4
1988	4.7
1989	6.6
1990	17.6
1991	28.6
1992	4.0
1993	16.7
1994	17.8
Average	14.0

Source: World Bank (1997, p. 80).

The implications of the Guarantee Reserve are also interesting. Since approximately 1% of the accumulation in the AFP is put into the Guarantee Reserve, the longer the AFP operates in the market the larger the Reserve becomes. When a new customer is searching for an AFP to join, a large Guarantee Reserve is an attractive attribute. A bigger reserve means that the AFP is more capable of making aggressive investments. These yield higher-than-average expected returns. Any losses that may occur are covered by the reserve. Thus, the existing reserve can benefit new customers, even though it has been accumulated through the contributions of older members. Given this situation, potential new entrants into the AFP market will find it hard to compete with AFPs that have existed for some time. This limits the degree of competition in the market and is not conducive to lowering the administrative costs of the AFPs.

Despite the problems associated with the design of the Chilean system, its achievements have been impressive. Total funds accumulated in the individual accounts have been growing at an average rate of 40% per year. By July 1994 the total stock was valued at

Table 4.2

Real Rate of Return for Private Pension Funds in Several Countries (1970–90)

Country	Rate of Return (%)
Canada	2.2
Denmark	4.1
Germany	5.1
Japan	4.4
Netherlands	4.2
Switzerland	1.2
United Kingdom	6.1
United States	3.3
Average	3.8

Source: World Bank (1997, p. 80).

US$ 22.3 billion, or 43% of the GDP. The system has also become a major source of private savings. In 1994 it accounted for 35% of national savings (World Bank 1996 Box 4.1). The number of people joining the system is also large. By September 1993, 93.4% of the workforce, or 4,553,988 people, were already members of AFPs (International Labour Office 1994). The attractiveness of the Chilean system has probably been mainly the result of the high rate of returns. As Table 4.1 indicates, the average real rate of returns from 1981 to 1994 was an impressive 14%.

The average rate of return for Chile's AFPs compares very well with the rates achieved in other countries. Table 4.2 shows that the unweighted simple average real rate of return for the private pension funds in several industrial countries was a significant but less-impressive 3.8%.[5] Chile's high average rate of return may in part be due to its economic reform and rapid growth in the same period. It is probable that its achievement is not sustainable in the long run.

The success of Chile's pension reform has made it a role model for many other countries. Several factors seem to account for the success. First, the system allows small amounts of private savings to be aggregated into large pension-fund pools. This opens up new investment opportunities that were previously unavailable to small investors. A number of investment strategies, such as hedging for currency risks, diversification, and taking advantage of economies of scale, are now possible. Second, the pension reform has been progressing hand in hand with Chile's economic reform. In particular, economic efficiency appears to have been significantly enhanced since the reform started. This has helped reduce political opposition to the new system. Third, the PAYG system was obviously in trouble before the introduction of the AFP. The large implicit debt of the former and the falling support ratio made it less certain that people would be able to obtain the pension benefits they expected after retirement. A change was called for. Fourth, the system was able to provide good insulation against political risks, such as the pressure to use it as a means for income redistribution or as a source to fund government budget deficits (Diamond 1994). Fifth, as we shall see in the next (third) section of this chapter, the Chilean government was able to resolve one of the most difficult problems of the reform, that is, financing the compensation of those who had already paid taxes for the PAYG system.

Phasing Out the PAYG System

One of the most valuable lessons we can learn from the Chilean experience is that of how it phased out the PAYG social security system. This was a difficult but important task. As discussed in Chapter 2, the design of a PAYG system is such that social security tax payments made by the working population are almost immediately spent on old people. If the system is abolished there will be no more tax proceeds with which to repay those who contributed previously. The resulting political pressure may make the transition to a new scheme very difficult.

The fundamental problem that the Chilean government had to resolve was that of how to repay the PAYG system's implicit debt. As discussed in the first section, the debt amounted to about 80% of the GDP before the reform started. The government's financial constraints made it impossible to finance all the compensations with just one lump-sum payment. The Chilean government therefore resorted to spreading out the burden. The main instrument it used was the issue of a new government security known as recognition bonds.

Workers who had contributed to the PAYG system for at least twelve months during the five years prior to November 1980 could receive recognition bonds representing the value of their accrued rights in the old system, provided that they were willing to switch over to the private pension fund.[6] The value of the bonds received would be calculated using a well defined formula. Eighty per cent of the insured's total earnings in the twelve months before June 1979, after adjustment for inflation, was assumed to be the annual income. This was then multiplied by the number of years of work, up to a maximum of thirty-five years. This method of calculating total lifetime earnings could resolve the problem of dealing with incomplete records of workers' earnings early in their careers. The amount was multiplied by a factor of 10.35 for men and 11.36 for women and was then divided by 35. The result was further adjusted by multiplying it by a factor of between 1 and 1.3, depending on the age of the worker at the time of switching. Old workers got a higher factor.

Recognition bonds are redeemable when a worker retires. They carry a real interest rate of 4% per year. The bonds are issued in the name of the worker and are placed under the custody of the pension-fund management company. They are portable in the sense that if the worker chooses a new fund, they can be transferred to the latter together with the remaining balance in the old fund.

The bonds and their interest payments are funded entirely by general government revenues. For the first ten years following the reform an annual cash flow of approximately 5% of the GDP was needed to finance the transition gap. For the next twenty years the expense of redeeming the recognition bonds was estimated at about 1% of the GDP. The Chilean government was experiencing a budget surplus of 5.5% of GDP in the first year of the reform, which made the transition easier. This was achieved in part by selling state-owned enterprises in the market. In subsequent years the government was not always able to maintain the surplus. However,

Table 4.3

Chilean Private Pension Funds: Operating Costs as Percentage of Total Assets

Year	Operating Costs (%)
1981	14.3
1982	7.3
1983	5.6
1984	4.1
1985	3.4
1986	2.9
1987	2.9
1988	2.8
1989	2.3
1990	1.8
1991	1.9

Source: World Bank (1997, p. 80).

if pension expenditures were excluded from the budget a surplus would still persist. Other means of saving money included improving the administrative efficiency of the government and raising the retirement age of men to sixty-five and of women to sixty. Moreover, since the creation of private pension funds, the government had been able to raise money by selling bonds to these funds.

In order to attract more people to join the privatized AFP the government decreed that employers had to grant a one-time 18% increase in the nominal wage rate. This was roughly equivalent to a real increase of 11%. This was considered necessary because employee contribution to the pension system was higher than it had been in the old system.

Administrative Costs

A common criticism of the Chilean private pension system is that it incurs high administrative or operating costs. As indicated in Table 4.3, operating costs as a percentage of total assets value were at a 14.3% peak in 1981, the first year after the system had been put into place. The costs then rapidly declined. In the 1990s they were less than 2%. The high initial costs could have been due partly to economies of scale and were not long lasting. However, administrative costs at the 2% level should still be considered very high. In fact, it is not uncommon to find pension funds in better-developed financial markets that charge a substantially lower rate.[7] Why have operating costs been so high in the Chilean system? There seem to be four reasons explaining this. (See Diamond and Valdes-Prieto (1994) for more detailed discussions.)

First, entry costs of new AFPs appear to be very high. Learning by doing seems to have been taking place on an industry-wide basis. This may be one of the reasons that administrative costs have been going down over time.

Second, each AFP is restricted to managing only a single pension fund. If a worker decides to switch to another type of fund, he is forced to join another AFP. The unavailability of internal switching means that unnecessary costs are involved in terminating the account in the old AFP and creating another account in the new AFP.

Third, under the system each AFP has to collect its own contributions separately, although some AFPs have signed service contracts with banks so that the latter will perform the tasks on their behalf. When the electronic system for collection is not well developed, the process can be cumbersome and costly. This is why some firms have tried to encourage all their workers to choose the same AFP. This problem, however, has a simple solution. If a central clearinghouse were established then employers could avoid the nuisance of making payments to a large number of AFPs. The latter also would not have to deal with many employers at the same time. Transaction costs could be expected to decline substantially.

Fourth, the Fluctuating Profit Reserve and the Guarantee Reserve, which are meant to provide a minimum rate of return to pension-fund investments, could become entry barriers for new AFPs. AFPs that have been in existence for a long time are more likely to have accumulated enough reserves to avoid being dissolved by the SAFP. New AFPs, lacking these two types of reserves, may not have the capacity to guarantee the required minimum rate of return. They are less attractive to pensioners. This weakens the threat of potential new entrants and lowers the degree of competition in the system. When existing AFPs are able to maintain some monopoly influence, they have less incentive to reduce fees.

Thus, there appear to be a number of factors contributing to the high administrative fees in Chile's pension-fund system. Other countries that attempt to adopt a similar plan need to consider ways to resolve these problems. Otherwise, the reduction in the rate of return caused by the high fees can significantly erode the living standard of the retired.

Private Pension Funds in Other Countries

Chile's successful transition from a PAYG system to one based on privatized fully funded pensions has made it a model that many others have followed. After more than ten years of observation, Latin American countries such as Peru, Colombia, Argentina, Bolivia, Mexico, El Salvador, and Uruguay have one after another adopted some elements of the Chilean system.[8] Its influence has not been confined to Latin America, either. Some European countries, long burdened by their obligation to finance the PAYG system, have also learned from Chile's experience. Italy, for example, has set up a regulatory framework enabling a privatized pension scheme to function (Kielmas 1995). Hungary and Poland have also passed legislation to introduce compulsory private pension arrangements (Batty 1997). In this section I briefly compare the new private pension systems in a few of these countries. This will show us how these countries have modified the Chilean system to suit their own needs.

Peru

Peru's pension system, or the AFP, which began to operate in May 1993, is very closely modelled on the Chilean system. Like workers in Chile, Peruvian workers are given the option of choosing between staying with the old PAYG system or switching to the private system. If they decide to join the new system, their employers must give them a one-time pay increase, just as employers in Chile must do for their workers. In this case, the pay rise is 13.23% of the salary. Peru has also learned from Chile to issue recognition bonds to resolve the transition problem. Moreover, as in Chile, employers do not make any contributions to the new system, and employees contribute at a similar rate. They have to pay 10% of their salary for old-age retirement, 1.5% for disability and survivor insurance, and 2% for administrative charges.

There are also differences. The value of recognition bonds received cannot exceed 60,000 soles (approximately US$ 30,000). They do not carry any interest payments. These measures are meant to reduce the costs of phasing out the old system. There is also no guaranteed minimum pension for the private system.

Argentina

Inspired by Chile, Argentina also instituted a private pension system in September 1993. However, the hand of the government is much more visible here, and the system is only partially private. Law No. 24241 establishes an "Integrated Retirement and Pension Scheme" that consists of both a PAYG system and a fully funded scheme. It is mandatory for the workers to join both. The latter is run by the Administradoras de Fondos de Jubilaciones y Pensiones (AFJP). The state-owned Banco de la Nacion Argentina is also included as one of the AFJPs, and it targets a large number of workers. This waters down the private nature of the pension-fund system.

The total contribution rate is also higher in Argentina than the rate in Chile. Employers pay 16% of wages and workers 11%. There is no guaranteed minimum pension. However, an AFJP Superintendent does try to streamline the system to ensure that the rate of return does not fall below a certain minimum.

Colombia

The retirement system in Colombia, known as the "Integrated Social Security Scheme," was established in December 1993. Under this system workers can choose between two types of pension schemes, a publicly run "solidarity scheme" or a privately managed "individual retirement scheme with solidarity".[9] For each scheme the total contribution rate in 1996 was 13.5% of the wage rate, of which 3.5 percentage points went to disability and survivors' benefits. Employers have to pay 75% of the total contribution. In contrast to the Chilean system, in Columbia the pension fund incorporates an income redistributive element. Workers earning a wage rate at least four times the minimum wage have to pay an extra 1% of the wages to a solidarity fund.

Bolivia

Bolivia's privatized pension scheme began operation in 1997. As in some Latin American countries, Bolivian workers have to contribute 10% of their wages to an old-age pension. They have the freedom to choose account managers and to switch from one fund to another annually. All new entrants to the labour force must join the private pension scheme, but older workers have the option of staying with the PAYG system. Those who decide to leave the old scheme will no longer be eligible to receive any benefits from it. Transition devices, like recognition bonds, have not been adopted here. Those who stay with the old system are guaranteed US$200 a year upon retirement. It seems likely that older or poorer workers will choose the PAYG system, whereas the younger and better off ones will join the private scheme.

The most important characteristic of the Bolivian system is that the government has sold six leading state-owned enterprises to help resolve the financial difficulties associated with retirement protection. Half of the proceeds from the privatization are deposited in the private individual pension accounts of those over the age of twenty-one. The remaining proceeds go to the financing of the PAYG system. It seems that the government wants to take an impartial position with regard to which system it should support. The selling of state-owned enterprises is yet another innovative approach to dealing with the transition problem.

This chapter discusses some of pertinent issues related to the celebrated Chilean privatized pension system. We have reviewed the scheme's remarkable achievements and the new problems that have been created. The historical significance of the Chilean system is that it has been able to ameliorate the tremendous financial impact involved with phasing out a PAYG system. This makes the implementation of pension reforms politically possible and financially practical.

It is hardly a surprise that many other countries have followed Chile's lead. In the process these countries have also modified some rules to suit their own needs. The degree of privatization varies from one country to another. Innovations have emerged as well. Some of these innovations, such as Bolivia's decision to generate funds by selling state-owned enterprises, can serve as sources of inspiration for other countries contemplating pension reforms. In refining its steps towards the creation of a new pension scheme, Hong Kong stands to learn a lot from the experiences of these countries.

Notes

1. This section follows Kritzer (1996a) closely.

2. See Chapter 2 for a fuller discussion on the dependency-ratio issue.

3. Appendix 1 provides a formula for the computation of benefits.

4. Details of the role of the state are discussed in World Bank (1996), Annex 3.1.

5. Also see Table 3.2 of Chapter 3.

6. This section draws materials from World Bank (1996a), Vittas (1995), and Kritzer (1996a).

7. For example, the largest retirement fund in the United States, TIAA-CREF, charges a fee of 0.31% in its common stock account. See its Web site for details.

8. See *International Labour Review* (1994), Kritzer (1996b, 1997), Case (1998), and Hinchberger (1998) for details. This section draws materials heavily from these papers.

9. In this respect the Colombia scheme is similar to a system in which a CPF and private pension funds exist. This scenario has attracted some interest in the debate about the retirement system in Hong Kong.

CHAPTER 5

What Retirement Plan Does Hong Kong Need?

In this chapter I examine some specific factors relevant to designing a viable and sustainable retirement-protection scheme for Hong Kong. Although I have already provided general evaluations of the PAYG system, the CPF, and the Chilean-style private pension fund, it is still necessary to consider Hong Kong's special conditions when I try to determine the best retirement-protection system for the city. For example, we know that the PAYG system is more likely to be optimal if the number of younger people exceeds that of older people for every generation, and vice versa. Thus, in assessing this scheme, we need to understand Hong Kong's population structure.

This chapter is divided into five parts. We begin by examining the demographics of Hong Kong. We shall see how this severely constrains our choice of a retirement plan. In the second section some economic features of Hong Kong are discussed. These again help us determine what a viable plan for Hong Kong should be like. The fully funded system is scrutinized in the third section. Pension benefits are projected under different scenarios and the results are compared to those in a PAYG system. I also show that a mandatory private pension system dominates a CPF. The fourth section presents some arguments against the use of a private pension system. I show how the scheme should be modified and supplemented in view of the valid points made in the arguments. Finally, some details of the legislation related to the MPF of the Hong Kong SAR Government are discussed in the last section. Suggestions for improvement are proposed.

Chapter 5

Table 5.1

Population Structure of Hong Kong, 1996 and 2036

Age	% of Population 1996	% of Population 2036
0 – 4	5.97	2.72
5 – 9	6.12	3.05
10 – 14	6.82	3.35
15 – 19	6.73	3.60
20 – 24	7.32	3.83
25 – 29	8.44	4.18
30 – 34	10.37	4.80
35 – 39	10.51	5.49
40 – 44	8.51	6.50
45 – 49	6.96	6.65
50 – 54	4.13	7.34
55 – 59	4.03	7.13
60 – 64	4.10	7.54
65 – 69	3.63	8.34
70 – 74	2.75	9.46
75+	3.63	16.02

Source: 1996 data are based on the by-census of that year. See endnote 7 for the assumptions behind the 2036 figures.

Features of Hong Kong's Demographic Structure, and Its Relationship to a PAYG System

The viability of the PAYG scheme as a retirement-protection system for Hong Kong depends critically on the city's demographic structure. Two features in particular can tell us a lot about what has been happening to Hong Kong's population. First, during the last several decades we have seen a persistently declining trend in the total fertility rate, which is defined as the number of children that a woman is expected to bear in her entire lifetime (given the current fertility rates of women of different age cohorts). In 1965 the total fertility rate was 4.5. It then declined to 3.3 in 1970, to 2.0 in 1980, to 1.4 in 1991, and, according to the most recent population by-census, to less than 1.19 in 1996.[1] This rate, which is well below the world's average of 2.9, ranks with the rates of Spain, Germany, and Italy as one of the four lowest in the world.[2] We see no clear sign indicating that the trend will reverse in the near future, even though there have been large increases in the number of immigrants from China to

Figure 5.1
Percentage of Hong Kong Population by Age Group, 1996

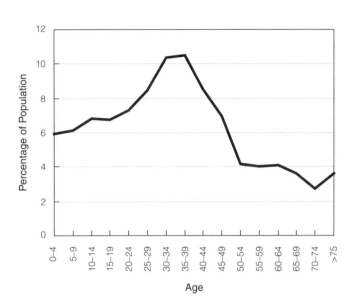

Hong Kong in recent years. Second, Hong Kong's people tend to live for a long time. In 1982 life expectancy at birth had already reached seventy-five years. In 1989 it rose to seventy-eight years and in 1996 to seventy-nine.[3] Casual reading of *The World Development Report 1997* clearly shows that Hong Kong, Japan, and Sweden, are the three places in the world with the highest life expectancy.[4] These facts have inevitably contributed to the ageing of the population of Hong Kong. In 1986 the median age of the population was twenty-eight. In 1991 it rose to thirty-one and in 1996 to thirty-four.[5]

The statistics summarized above have far-reaching consequences for a PAYG system. These can be understood more clearly if we use another tool to characterize the population structure. Column 2 of Table 5.1 presents the 1996 by-census data on the percentage of the population at each age cohort. Figure 5.1 shows the same relationship, but in graphical form.[6] As is evident from the table and the diagram, a large proportion of people in Hong Kong are aged between twenty-five and forty-nine. This must be

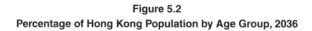

Figure 5.2
Percentage of Hong Kong Population by Age Group, 2036

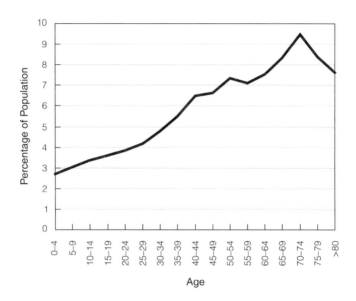

due to the fact that the total fertility rate was very high during the baby-boom period several decades ago. The proportion of young people is smaller but still substantial, despite the very low total fertility rate in recent years. This can be attributed to the fact that the number of women at childbearing age has been large, even though each of them does not give birth to many children. The proportion of old people in society as a whole is much smaller than that of younger working adults.

If a PAYG system had been adopted in 1996 it is unlikely that the social security tax rate would have to be very high, simply because there would have been more young taxpayers than retired people whom they had to support. However, Figure 5.1 also implies that in three or four decades the situation will change drastically. Most of the old people of today will disappear from the population, and many working adults will retire. Today's children will also become working adults. If the PAYG system were still in place at

Table 5.2
Support Ratio in Hong Kong, 1996–2046

Age	Support Ratio
1996	7.10
2001	6.00
2006	5.84
2011	5.63
2016	4.53
2021	3.49
2026	2.53
2031	1.94
2036	1.69
2041	1.61
2046	1.55

Source: Based on 1996 population by-Census data. See also endnote 7.

that time it would be necessary to impose a high tax rate in order to maintain a decent level of benefits. Alternatively, if political pressure would prohibit too high a tax rate, the benefits level would have to decrease.

The above analysis is compatible with the projected population structure of the year 2036, which is presented in Table 5.1 and graphically in Figure 5.2.[7] The proportion of old people increases significantly, whereas that of the young clearly goes down. This pattern is similar to the so-called inverted population pyramid in the demography literature referring to an ageing population. Alternatively, we can use the concept of the support ratio to articulate what will happen to the population structure.

Support ratio is defined as the percentage of the population aged between fifteen and sixty-four divided by the percentage of the population aged sixty-five or above. It can readily be seen that the support ratio declines rapidly from 7.10 in 1996 to 1.69 in 2036 (see Table 5.2 and Figure 5.3). This means that in the future there will be fewer and fewer young people who can pay taxes to support the old. In fact, to be more precise, the proportion of taxpayers to PAYG benefits recipients in, say, 2036, will be less than 1.69. This is

Figure 5.3
Support Ratio of Hong Kong, 1996–2046

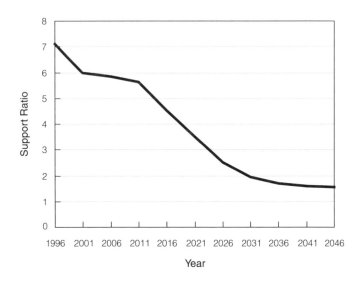

because not everybody within the fifteen to sixty-four-year-old age group works. Since the labour force participation rate for people in this age group is around 0.68, there will only be 1.15 taxpayers supporting each person receiving social security benefits.[8] Thus, if a PAYG system were to be adopted, either the tax rate would increase over time or the benefit level would decrease. However, the negative effect of the declining support ratio could possibly be mitigated by a sufficiently rapid real-wage growth rate because the PAYG system typically taxes the wage income to finance its expenditures. In other words, if the wage rate increases quickly, then in the future there will be more tax revenues to support the retirement benefits of old people. To properly evaluate the viability of the PAYG system for Hong Kong, we need to consider factors that may affect growth of the wage rate. The next section addresses this viability issue. The third section of this chapter will take the various parameters of an alternative scheme into account quantitatively, and it will be shown that the situation discussed above applies.

Why the PAYG System is Not Suitable for Hong Kong

In the previous section I demonstrate that the support ratio in Hong Kong will continue to decline in the next few decades. As I will show in the next section, this will effectively lower the PAYG system's implicit rate of return. This effect is particularly pronounced in Hong Kong because the support ratio will change so dramatically as time passes. For this reason alone, the PAYG system is not an acceptable retirement plan for Hong Kong. However, demography is far from the only factor that has been raised in arguments against adopting the PAYG system. The objections, many of which were voiced by economists when the plan was proposed by the government in 1994, go much deeper.[9] In this section I discuss a few of the more important objections.

First, as discussed in Chapter 2, a PAYG system generally depresses the growth rate of an economy, provided that the economy's fertility rate is at such a low level that it cannot go down much further. In the case of Hong Kong, the fertility rate is already very low. So the PAYG system's effect on the economic growth rate would be negative. Conservative calculations based on the estimated parameters in Ehrlich and Lui (1998) show that the reduction in the long-term real growth rate of Hong Kong's GDP could reach 0.36 of a percentage point if a PAYG system were adopted. The total accumulated foregone losses in, say, forty years, would be enormous even when the decrease in the long-term growth rate were minor. In fact, given that the growth rate would be reduced by 0.36 percentage points, the total losses over forty years would amount to HK$11,000 billion in real terms, which is more than eight years of the GDP of Hong Kong.[10] Although this is only a crude estimation, the sheer size of the loss clearly indicates that the PAYG system is not an optimal scheme for Hong Kong.

Second, the PAYG system relies on taxing wage income to finance social security benefits. If the average wage rate in the economy grows very slowly, the expected benefits after retirement, or the implicit rate of return of the PAYG system, must be very low.

Government statistics show that the growth rate in average real wages in Hong Kong since 1990 has been staying at about 0.5%.[11] This is far below the growth rate of the GDP itself. Will this pattern continue into the next century? To answer this question we have to understand why the pattern has been established in the first place. An important reason behind this is that the economic integration of Hong Kong with China has had a dampening effect on Hong Kong's wage rate. In Hong Kong capital is relatively abundant, but labour is relatively scarce, whereas China has little capital but many workers. China's economic reform has provided many profitable investment opportunities for Hong Kong businessmen in the Mainland. People who can provide capital will gain in such a situation. On the other hand, the virtually unlimited supply of labour in China has created a new pool of competitors for Hong Kong workers. This is unlikely to change in the near future, because investors can readily find new supplies of cheap labour as they move inland. Given these conditions, a retirement plan that is heavily influenced by the growth in the wage rate is unlikely to be a good choice, whereas a scheme that relies on capital investment should be able to yield more wealth. In this regard, a fully funded investment scheme is superior to the PAYG system for Hong Kong.

Third, one characteristic of a good retirement scheme is that the risks involved are not unduly high. The Hong Kong economy is relatively small and is subject to a high degree of volatility. In designing a retirement-protection scheme, it is natural that we consider ways to reduce the risks created by the fluctuations. If a fully funded system is adopted, then, in principle, the proceeds can be invested in different countries. Diversification of the investment portfolio will naturally reduce the risks. The PAYG system, on the other hand, anchors the rate of return to changes in the domestic labour market. If the labour market is not favourable for workers, then retirees' returns will not be as good. A city as dynamic as Hong Kong needs flexibility for making adjustments. The PAYG system is too restrictive to allow for sufficient diversification.

Some supporters of the PAYG system argue that a fully funded retirement plan, such as the CPF or the Chilean-style private pension fund, cannot provide enough coverage for old people. These must therefore be supplemented by a PAYG system, they say. While fully funded schemes have their pros and cons, they cannot resolve the difficulties of a PAYG system. From the perspective of resource allocation, one may question why any money should ever be spent on a scheme that reduces the economic growth rate and yields a lower rate of return. The fact that a pension fund coexists with it does not eliminate these difficulties. Taxes paid for the PAYG system could be more efficiently utilized if the money were contributed to a pension fund instead.[12]

A Mandatory Private Pension Plan for Hong Kong?

Although the PAYG system has to be excluded as a viable option in Hong Kong, this does not necessarily imply that a public retirement-protection scheme should not be established. The ageing of the population in Hong Kong, as reflected by the rapidly rising median age and the declining support ratio, has exerted significant political pressure on the government to resolve the problem of retirement protection. The most important alternatives to the PAYG system are the CPF and the mandatory private pension fund.[13] These two systems share the common feature of being fully funded investment plans. However, the poor performance of publicly managed pension plans documented in Table 3.2 makes the CPF an unattractive option. I shall therefore focus on the private scheme, now known as the MPF in Hong Kong.

Will the MPF provide enough protection for retirement? The answer depends on a number of parameters, including the projected long-run average rate of return, the real rate of increase in the salary, the contribution rate for the fund, the age at which participants join the fund, the retirement age, and the expected length of life after retirement. To make meaningful projection about the benefits of the MPF, I shall discuss each of these parameters and shall calibrate their values.

The expected long-term rate of return of a pension fund is one of the most difficult parameters to predict. Nevertheless, some educated estimates on the conservative side are still possible. From April 1964 to April 1998 the average annual nominal rate of return of the Hang Seng Index stocks was over 18%.[14] This implies a real rate of return of about 9% a year. The terminal month (1998) is used because the Hang Seng Index has largely reflected the impact of the worst currency crisis in Asia's post-World War II history. The performance of the Hang Seng Index is consistent with that of private pension funds. There are commercial enterprises that have been tracking the latter's performance in Hong Kong. During the eleven-year period from 1983 to 1994 the median average nominal rate of return of a representative sample of Hong Kong pension funds, according to a survey conducted by Wyatt (1995), was 16.3% per year. Inflation during this period was 8.8% per year. This gives an annual real rate of return of 7.5% a year. The terminal year of 1994 is chosen because that was an exceptionally bad year for the stock market in Hong Kong. The resulting rate of return therefore tends to be biased downwards.

Since the portfolio of a pension fund may include foreign exposure we should also look at the performance of foreign pension funds. Table 3.2 indicates that a real rate of return of over 8% a year is not unusual.[15] Although it is well known that past results do not guarantee future performance, it is reasonable to conjecture that so long as the long-term economic growth rates of Hong Kong or other major markets in the world do not decline significantly, comparable rates of return can be expected. In calculating pension benefits I assume that the real rate of return is 4% for the benchmark scenario and 7% for the less conservative scenario.

Another important parameter is the rate of increase in the salary. Here the growth rate of salary that should be tracked is conceptually different from that used for calculating the benefits of the PAYG system. In the latter case the benefits depend on the social security tax, which is imposed on the wages of all workers. We have to track the rate of increase of the average wage rate in the economy. To calculate the pension benefits of an individual who has joined a private fund, we must take into account the fact that the amount of the monthly contribution to the fund depends on the salary of that individual. Over time, his salary increases consist of two components, namely, the general rise in average wages across society, and his raises earned as a result of promotion or seniority. Thus, the annual growth in the salary of a person normally exceeds the increase in the average wage rate in the economy. I assume that the real growth rate of the salary is 3% a year.[16]

The other parameters can be determined more easily. The contribution rate is assumed to be 10% of the salary. This follows the legislative requirement of the MPF. The retirement age is taken to be sixty-five, and the expected length of retirement life is fifteen years. I also assume that after retirement, if a person so desires, he can buy an actuarially fair annuity using his entire accumulated MPF. The annuity will provide him with monthly payments, which are calculated based on the same rate of return as that which the MPF enjoys.

Table 5.3 presents the monthly benefits of the MPF in real terms as multiples of today's salary. These benefits are calculated using the parametric values assumed above and the formula in the Mathematical Appendix. Two scenarios are presented. In the first, the real rate of return is 4% a year, and in the second it is 7%.

As is obvious from Table 5.3, benefits of the MPF decline rather quickly as the age of entry increases. The benchmark scenario indicates that if a person joining the MPF at an age over forty-five relies *solely* on it, that is, he has no savings or other forms of retirement protection, and if his salary level is well below the median wage rate, then it will be difficult for him to maintain a decent retirement life. Even if the rate of return is 7%, those joining the MPF after the age of fifty will also find that the scheme alone will not provide enough old-age support. Thus, it may appear that the MPF cannot provide enough protection for a significant part of the current population. This is not surprising because, after all, the MPF is meant to provide retirement protection for the long run. There is also no need for undue concern about this issue because, even in the absence of the MPF, Hong Kong's gross domestic saving

Table 5.3

Real Monthly MPF Benefits as Multiples of Monthly Salary at the Age of Entry

Age of Joining MPF	Scenario 1 (4%)	Scenario 2 (7%)
20	1.87 times	4.76 times
25	1.40	3.24
30	1.03	2.18
35	0.74	1.43
40	0.52	0.92
45	0.35	0.57
50	0.22	0.33
55	0.12	0.17
60	0.05	0.07

Notes: Scenario 1 refers to the case in which the real rate of return of investment in the MPF is 4% a year. In scenario 2 it is 7% a year. Columns 2 and 3 show monthly pension benefits as multiples of the salary at the age of joining the MPF. For example, if the age of entry is 20, and the salary at that time is HK$10,000 per month, the monthly pension is expected to be HK$18,700 in real terms.

rate has remained at around 32% of income. A middle-aged person who had no savings at all would not be typical. Moreover, as time goes by, the average entry age into the MPF will become lower and lower. Nevertheless, it is still useful for us to consider ways to resolve the difficulty faced by those who are near retirement age but who have not saved enough. This will be discussed in the next section.

One may also raise the question of what will happen to MPF benefits if economic conditions turn bad. If the downturn is temporary its implications for MFP benefits will be insignificant. People can even take advantage of the situation by buying securities at low prices. If the deterioration is more permanent in nature, however, benefits will of course be affected. However, in such a situation, the performance of the PAYG system may be worse than that of the MPF because the former relies on taxing the wage income, which will likely be depressed at a time of economic stagnancy. In deciding whether the MPF is better than the PAYG system, we need to assume similar conditions for the two schemes and to compare their respective benefits.

Table 5.4

Comparison of Pension Benefits between MPF and PAYG Systems

Age of Entry	MPF (4%)	MPF (7%)	PAYG (Average Wage)	PAYG (Half of Average Wage)
20	1.87 times	4.76 times	0.25 times	0.50 times
25	1.40	3.24	0.24	0.48
30	1.03	2.18	0.25	0.51
35	0.74	1.43	0.30	0.60
40	0.52	0.92	0.37	0.74
45	0.35	0.57	0.44	0.88
50	0.22	0.33	0.49	0.99
55	0.12	0.17	0.46	0.93
60	0.05	0.07	0.43	0.86

Notes: Columns 1 to 3 are identical to Table 5.3. Columns 4 and 5 are the expected monthly PAYG benefits in the first year of retirement as multiples of the salary at the age of joining the scheme. Column 4 refers to the case in which the person's salary at the age of entry is equal to the average wage rate in the economy. Column 5 refers to the case in which the person's salary at the age of entry is only half of society's average wage rate. All salaries are in real terms.

In calculating the monthly benefits of the PAYG system it is necessary to make some assumptions. In particular, I assume that the tax rate is 10% of the salary. This is in line with the contribution rate for the MPF. The retirement age is sixty-five. We also need to know the support ratio in order to perform the calculations. Data from Table 5.2 are used for this purpose. The real rate of increase in the economy's average wage rate is taken to be 2% a year. As noted earlier in this chapter, this rate should be lower than the growth rate of an individual's salary.[17] Another assumption that needs to be made is that of the labour force participation rate. This is important because only a portion of the people aged between fifteen and sixty-four will pay social security taxes to support the retired.

Table 5.4 presents the comparison between the pension benefits of the MPF and the PAYG system under different scenarios. In the case of the PAYG scheme, there is an element of built-in income redistribution. It is assumed that every retiree receives the same benefits. Those whose salaries are lower will therefore gain more. The last two columns represent the monthly benefits as the number of times of the salary at the age of entry for those whose salaries are equal to the economy's average wage and half of the average age, respectively.

Examination of Table 5.4 readily shows that a person in his early forties will be somewhat indifferent between the two schemes if his salary is equal to the economy's average and if the MPF's expected rate of return is 4%. Younger people are likely to prefer the MPF, whereas older ones will probably prefer the PAYG system. If the expected rate of return for the MPF is 7%, then those who have passed their late forties may prefer the PAYG system. By reading the last column one can draw other conclusions for the poorer group of people whose wage rate is only half of the economy's average. The results again confirm the view that the older people of today can benefit more from the PAYG system. However, as time goes on and everybody is forced to join the system at a young age, very few people will gain.[18]

The results presented in this section indicate that so long as the person joining the MPF is not too old, the future benefits will be sufficient to support his retirement. The PAYG system, on the other hand, may generate some apparent windfall gain for the old people of today. They did not contribute to the system, but they can benefit from it. However, their gains are at the expense of future generations. The MPF does not share this problem. It is more robust than the PAYG system.

A More Comprehensive Retirement-Protection System

It is often argued that it takes too long for the MPF to become effective. Moreover, there is no income redistributive element built into it to provide immediate relief for the elderly poor. To the extent that the MPF is meant as a long-term retirement-protection plan, the criticism that it has little immediate effect is valid. It is also true that the plan, unlike the PAYG system, does not redistribute income.

However, we should not forget that the PAYG system is an inter-generational redistributive scheme whose beneficiaries are not necessarily poor. In this section I show that the MPF can provide the basis for a viable supplemental retirement-protection mechanism. The MPF, together with the supplemental scheme, form a comprehensive retirement-protection system that is not subject to the criticisms just mentioned.

To ensure that some income is channelled only to those with genuine needs, the supplemental programme has to be means tested. At present, the Hong Kong SAR Government has two main vehicles of welfare support for the elderly. The first is the Comprehensive Social Security Assistance programme (CSSA), which is means tested. The second is the Social Security Allowance (SSA), which is not means tested. The degree of support available from each of these is relatively low. From the government's point of view it is imprudent to significantly increase the benefits because that could signal an abandonment of the tradition of conservative fiscal policies characteristic of Hong Kong. The concern over "over-spending" is valid because (1) the number of old people will continue to increase, and (2) people will demand higher benefits as the real wage rate in society increases over time. A modest increase in the welfare budget today could mean much bigger changes in the future. In a successful plan, the welfare budget for the elderly should remain a relatively stable share of the GDP. It is here that the MPF can play an important role.

The decline in the support ratio over time increases the financial burden of providing welfare for the elderly. On the other hand, an important property of the MPF is that pension benefits will be larger the longer a person has been a member of the plan. When the welfare system has a means test, a smaller and smaller percentage of the aged population will be eligible for it. If we also deduct part of the welfare payment from the MPF benefits, then the welfare payment per recipient will possibly go down over time. In principle, these opposite effects on the financial burden can be manipulated so that they neutralize each other.

The basic ingredients of the comprehensive retirement protection system should therefore include the following.[19] First, the MPF should be in place. Second, the CSSA should continue to operate. Third, the criteria for passing CSSA's means test may be reviewed if necessary. However, once they are established they should be enforced. Fourth, MPF benefits, in the form of monthly payments, should be counted as incomes of the individuals.[20] The CSSA benefits for the eligible will have to be deducted to reflect this source of income. Fifth, total pension benefits (CSSA plus MPF) can be increased.

An objective of this system is to ensure that an improved social safety net as represented by the CSSA does not lead to the imposition of an excessive financial burden on the government. Such a burden will not become a problem if CSSA expenditures for the elderly remain a relatively stable, or even a declining, share of the GDP. To illustrate that this is achievable, I use a hypothetical example. It is admittedly a highly simplified version of actual conditions, but I hope that it contains enough truth to allow us to make use of it. A number of assumptions have to be made.

Currently the CSSA encompasses an array of welfare programmes. I focus on the means-tested programme for the elderly and ignore the others. In this chapter, I apply the term "CSSA" narrowly to this particular programme only. In 1998 the standard monthly rate of the CSSA for a person was HK$2,060.[21] A number of criteria on assets and income are used to determine eligibility. The age requirement is sixty years or older. In the hypothetical example I assume that the system started in 1996. This is because the by-census of that year gives us more reliable population and income data on which we can make our projections. I also assume that the initial CSSA payment, if not supplemented by the MPF, is HK$3,000 per month (in constant 1996 Hong Kong dollars). This amount is allowed to grow at 2% real per year. This substantial increase is meant to test the extent of the financial burden that the government has to bear. In July 1996 the number of people receiving the CSSA was 89,371 (Chow, 1996). This was equivalent to 10.2% of the population aged sixty and over. The hypothetical example assumes that the poorest 20% of the population who are at least sixty-five years old can get CSSA benefits. This is equivalent to around 126,000 people for 1996. To make possible a simplified and more conservative analysis, this percentage of eligible people is assumed not to decline over time.

According to statistics from the 1996 by-census those who made a total wage income of less than HK$6,000 a month constituted roughly 20% of the working population in that year. The average income of this group of people was about HK$3,850 a month.[22] This value is used to project the future MPF pension. The average rate of return for the MPF is 4% real per year. I also assume that the real wage rate goes up at a rate of 2% a year. An important consideration regarding MPF benefits is that people who do not participate in the labour force, including some housewives who do not accumulate money in their accounts. I assume that workers will use part of their MPF savings to support spouses who do not hold paying jobs. MPF support has been adjusted appropriately to reflect this.[23] As a result, such workers are eligible to receive more CSSA benefits.

To calculate CSSA expenditures we need to know the projected population figures for those aged at least sixty-five (Figure 5.4a). To determine these I have assumed that each year there will be in a net inflow of 55,000 immigrants into Hong Kong, the ages of whom are evenly distributed between zero and fifty-five. The last assumption is that real GDP grows at 3% per year. GDP data are from the Hong Kong Government (1998).

Results of the hypothetical example are presented in Table 5.5 and Figure 5.4. Column 6 is Column 4 minus Column 5 (Figure 5.4b). Column 7 is Column 6 times Column 3. The main result is embodied in the last column. In the hypothetical example CSSA expenditures do not necessarily go up faster than the GDP does. The ratio between the two (Column 8) remains relatively stable. It peaks at 2026 and then continues to decline (Figure 5.4c). This example shows that once the MPF is established it is feasible to increase CSSA benefits substantially without violating the principle of conservative fiscal policy. However, there must be a means test in order

Table 5.5
Hypothetical Elderly CSSA Expenditures as Percentage of GDP

Year (1)	Number of People over sixty-five (1,000) (2)	Number of CSSA Elderly Cases (1,000) (3)	Total Pension Needed (HK$) (4)	Support from MPF (HK$) (5)	Support from CSSA (HK$) (6)	CSSA Expend-tures (million HK$) (7)	CSSA as % of GDP (%) (8)
1996	632	126	36,000	0	36,000	4,536	0.38
2001	772	154	39,747	1,613	38,134	5,873	0.42
2006	811	162	43,884	3,835	40,049	6,488	0.40
2011	856	171	48,451	6,835	41,616	7,116	0.38
2016	1,041	208	53,494	10,828	42,666	8,875	0.41
2021	1,290	258	59,062	16,090	42,972	11,087	0.44
2026	1,628	326	65,209	22,956	42,253	13,774	0.48
2031	1,912	382	71,996	31,845	40,151	15,338	0.46
2036	2,033	407	79,489	43,286	36,203	14,735	0.38
2041	1,995	399	87,762	57,927	29,835	11,904	0.26

Note: CSSA recipients and expenditures apply only to those over sixty-five years of age. See
          text for explanations. Columns (4), (5), (6) are per case per year.

to make this outcome possible. This way, the MPF can lay the foundation for the provision of better CSSA benefits. It should be pointed out that the results are affected by the speed of increase in CSSA benefits. If CSSA benefits (Column 4), when not supplemented by the MPF, grow at a substantially faster rate than the rate of increase in the wages, then CSSA expenditures as a percentage of GDP will continue to go up. On the other hand, if the needed pensions in Column 4 grow at a slower rate, say, at 1% a year, then beginning in the year 2041 MPF pensions will be more than sufficient to cover not only retired workers but also their spouses.

Hong Kong's Newly Established MPF

On 1 April 1998 the Provisional Legislative Council of Hong Kong passed all the remaining legislative details of the MPF. Two days later it approved an allocation of HK$5 billion to establish the Mandatory Provident Fund Authority (MPFA). The MPF is now official. It is expected that its operation will commence in 1999 or 2000, if further lobbying attempts to delay it do not succeed. Some salient elements of the scheme are as follow.[24]

Figure 5.4
Hong Kong's Pension Needs, 1996–2041

a. Population 65+ and Elderly
   Welfare Cases

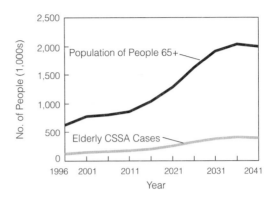

b. Private, Public and
   Total Amount of
   Pension Needed

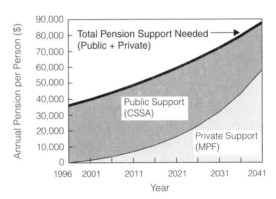

c. Welfare (CSSA) Expenditure
   as Percentage of GDP

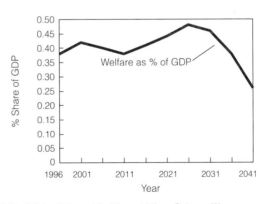

Sources: a. Column (2) and (3) of Table 5.5; b. Column (4), (5), and (6); c. Column (8).

Salient Elements of the MPF Scheme

Once the MPF begins to operate formally, with the exception of those who have special exemptions, all employers must contribute to an MPF scheme on behalf of their employees 5% of the employees' salary. The latter also have to contribute 5%. Thus, under normal circumstances, the forced saving rate of an employee is 10% of his or her salary. The employee contribution has a floor and a ceiling. Employees earning less than HK$4,000 a month do not have to contribute. Salary in excess of HK$20,000 a month is also exempted from the 5% contribution, if the employee desires it to be. Self-employed persons are subject to the same rules as are employees, that is, they have to contribute 5% of their income to the MPF.

Employers are responsible for choosing schemes on behalf of the employees. All schemes must be instituted as trust arrangements. The assets in such an arrangement are legally held by the trustee, but the benefits are vested in the trust members. If an employee changes jobs, he or she can choose to transfer the accrued benefits from the old scheme to the one appointed by the new employer. Thus, the MPF has a certain degree of portability.

The employee cannot withdraw the accrued benefits before retirement age. In case he or she has not attained retirement age but has reached the age of sixty, it may be possible for the employee to withdraw the benefits if he or she can certify that employment or self-employment has permanently ceased. The accrued assets are not to be subject to any charge, pledge, lien, mortgage, or other encumbrance except under some special circumstances. This means that people cannot borrow against assets in the MPF. Therefore, under normal conditions the 10% saving rate is in effect enforced.

Some Major Issues Faced by the MPF Authority

From the government's standpoint there are three issues related to the MPF that seem politically important. First, it must pay special attention to the security of the invested assets. Any losses in MPF investments due to fraud or excessive risk exposure, no matter how small these losses are, could give rise to a distrust of the regulatory framework of the MPF system and could stir up a sense discontentment with the government. Second, investors are often concerned that they may be paying too much for the administrative fees of the MPF. This concern is legitimate because small differences in the fees can significantly affect the monthly benefits of retirees. The problem is aggravated by the fact that employees are coerced into participating in the MPF. Third, it is sometimes believed that low-income people are especially vulnerable to investment risks and therefore need extra protection. One could substantiate this claim by arguing that poor people are less informed about the securities market and that the fixed costs of investing constitute a large percentage of the returns from relatively small investments. Moreover, these people's labour mobility is higher than average. Substantial costs can be incurred when funds are transferred in the process of a job change. Whether this is true or not is probably immaterial. Political reality will inevitably exert pressure on the government to establish various means targeted at protecting the poor.

The government has made some efforts to deal with the above-mentioned issues. The more important steps are summarized below.[25]

Security of Scheme Assets

The government adopts trusteeship arrangement for all MPF schemes. Assets accumulated in a scheme are legally held by its trustee, but members of the scheme own the benefits. The trustee of an MPF scheme must comply with the law and perform duties specified in the regulations and rules written by the MPF Authority. Violations could result in fines or prosecutions. The trustees must meet certain minimum requirements and must obtain prior approval from the MPF Authority in order to qualify to conduct MPF business. Investment managers must be incorporated in Hong Kong with capital and net assets above some minimum requirements.

To provide sufficient flexibility in investment strategies and at the same time to avoid excessive risk exposure, the government has prescribed a list of permissible investments. Moreover, the MPF

Authority, after consultation with the financial secretary, can prohibit some risky investment practices that may appear in the market in the future.

Some people have argued that MPF schemes should guarantee a minimum rate of return for their investments. It is well known that if such a guarantee exists, fund managers will be induced to invest only in safe assets with a very low expected rate of return. The resulting rate of return will be too low to be acceptable. Hong Kong's MPF system adopts another approach. Instead of imposing the guarantee, all schemes are required to provide a "capital preservation product". Investment of the fund will follow some very stringent restrictions. The rate of return will be low. Investors have some degree of freedom in deciding whether to join this fund. This approach is superior to providing a guarantee in the sense that it allows for greater consumer choice.

It is probably true that all regulatory systems have loopholes. An important supplementary safeguard against frauds and investment risks is to make the MPF transparent. Investors, who have more incentive than the government to protect their own assets, will be thus better able to monitor the funds' performance. The MPF Authority requires every trustee to compile a report each year showing an analysis of the investments made. The report has to be verified by external auditors. The MPF Authority will review the reports and annual accounts submitted. It also will carry out on-site inspections to monitor performance. In serious cases, the authority may appoint inspectors to perform in-depth investigations. Each year it will publish a report that includes a compilation of the investment statistics of all MPF funds. Investors, possibly aided by the proliferation of media information, can make their own comparisons. Another means to improving transparency is that of requiring trustees and employers to disclose sufficient information for employees. The latter will be aware of the amount of contributions deducted from their salary and will receive annual benefit statements. The schemes have to set up facilities whereby employees can find out their benefit entitlements. Employees can also file complaints and inquiries with the MPF Authority.

There are several insurance schemes designed to provide better security of scheme assets. First, an individual trustee must be covered by an adequate performance guarantee. If he fails to perform his duties, and if this results in investment losses, the insurance policy or a bank bond will have to pay the MPF Authority an amount for which he is personally liable. Second, the trustee of a scheme must purchase indemnity insurance to cover for losses in scheme assets due to misfeasance and illegal conduct by the trustee or by other service providers. Third, a compensation fund will be set up to compensate scheme members for losses resulting from illegal conduct or misfeasance. The losses to a scheme will first be covered by resources of the trustee and service providers, the performance guarantee, and the indemnity insurance. The compensation fund will be the last resort, provided that the MPF Authority can obtain approval from the court to use it.

Administrative Fees

In the debate over whether the CPF is superior to the privatized MPF, it is often claimed that the former will incur lower administrative costs. This is because under the CPF small companies do not need to set up their own retirement plans. All they have to do is deposit money into one big CPF. Economies of scale will help lower their costs. Moreover, when employees change jobs, they need not transfer funds or create new accounts. These seemingly advantageous features of the CPF can easily be captured by the MPF if the latter is properly designed. The MPF system in Hong Kong has to some extent moved in this direction.

The principal means to reducing the costs associated with the MPF for small enterprises is to establish "master trust" schemes. Under this arrangement, small schemes can be pooled together under a master trust for administration and investment. This method makes a lot of sense in the context of the current employer-based MPF schemes. However, as we shall see later, if the system is employee based, that is, if individual employees have the option of choosing their own preferred schemes to join, then the advantage offered by the master trust is much less apparent.

Competition is often the most powerful method used to reduce costs. The MPF Authority recognizes this and has built some elements of competition into the system. Service providers are not subject to any quota. Any individual or company satisfying the approval criteria, which are not overly stringent, can become an eligible MPF trustee. This is meant to remove barriers for entry into the market. The efforts made to increase the transparency and to improve the reporting system of each fund facilitate better decision making on the part of scheme members. This in turn forces some trustees to lower costs.

Since the MPF Authority is a government regulatory body, people may suspect that its expenditures, which ultimately have to be shared by scheme members, could rise to an unacceptable level. To prevent this from happening several measures have been undertaken. First, an initial HK$5 billion has been injected into the MPF Authority. It will become a self-financing entity. The additional fees paid by the scheme members to support its operations will be kept minimal. Second, the authority will be a slim establishment. Third, funds for protecting members from undue risks will rely mainly on the Indemnity Insurance and Compensation Fund, not on the authority itself.

There are other measures aimed at cutting administrative costs of the schemes. An automatic reporting mechanism has been set up to identify default contributions. The MPF Authority has the responsibility to prosecute default parties and to recover default contributions. Self-employed people who choose to pay the upper limit of HK$1000 a month do not have to produce verifications of their incomes. Procedures for transferring accrued benefits will be streamlined. Service providers are encouraged to use modern information technology to facilitate easier reporting, enrolment into the plan, and better communication.

Protecting the Low-Income Group

Some of the measures discussed can help protect low-income people. For example, the master trust arrangement is relevant for the poor who work in small companies. There are other mechanisms specifically designed for the purpose of protecting this segment of the population. The more important examples are as follows.

Some people believe that certain trustees do not want to accept low income workers into their plans because such workers' contributions are too small. The MPF has a statutory requirement stating that trustees cannot reject any persons who want to join their schemes, regardless of these individuals' income level.

The number of job changes among low income people is higher than average. Two things could result from this. If a worker does not transfer the accrued benefits from the account associated with the old employer to the one associated with the new one, then too many scattered accounts will be created. Second, if the worker does make the transfer, the costs involved, especially when there are many transfers, may deplete the future benefits.

A number of methods to resolve these issues have been proposed. First, industry schemes are to be set up for industries that have a high degree of intraindustry mobility. Second, the administrative process for transfers is to be made simple so that less cost will be incurred. Third, the MPF Authority will set up a mechanism to help scheme members trace the whereabouts of accounts they have forgotten. Fourth, no fees can be charged for moving an account. Actual expenses incurred for the redemption of investments are exempted from this restriction, however. If the balance in the account is HK$5,000 or less, redemption fees cannot be imposed, provided that the transfer occurs within a year after the account has become dormant. Fifth, trustees are required to remind scheme members to transfer or consolidate their accounts at the time of job changes.

Moral Hazard and Competition

MPF schemes are presently employer based. In other words, employees have to join the schemes that their employers have chosen for them. In the initial phase, when the general public has not acquired sufficient information about the MPF, this arrangement has the advantage of being simple. Employees will not be confused about what scheme to choose. However, in the long run, after people gradually come to understand more about the MPF mechanism, the disadvantages of the employer-based arrangement will become apparent.

Perhaps the most important shortcoming of this arrangement is that it will result in moral hazard behaviour on the part of employers. We know that the accrued benefits in the MPF belong to employees. Employers, however, choose the schemes. Are they motivated to choose the best managed scheme? There are many attributes of a scheme that a member has to consider. He has to know the long-term performance of the managed funds. He prefers a scheme that has lower administrative costs. Security and reliability are of course important. The information reporting system should be modern and convenient, and so on. Employers may indeed have some incentive to choose a "good" scheme, since doing so will enhance the image of the companies. However, it is also clear that the benefits and concerns of the employers and employees are not the same. Moreover, even among employees themselves, objectives and preferences may be different. A likely outcome of the employer-based scheme is that service providers who have been established in Hong Kong for a long time will be chosen. As long as the company does not have a bad name, the employers will believe that in choosing a reputable company, they have done all they need to fulfil their duty. Whether the performance of the scheme is mediocre or not is not very important to them.

If this phenomenon persists, some unintended market barriers will be created. International fund houses will find it harder to enter into the Hong Kong pension market. At the early stage of the public debate about the MPF some lobbyists against the plan argued that the annual administrative fees would amount to 5% or 6% of total assets. Fund managers, who were eager to see the MPF legislation go through, told the public that the fees would be much lower. The assumed benchmark rate was around 1.5%. Is this rate reasonable? Casual observations of pension programmes in other countries clearly indicate that it is on the high side. It is easy to find examples of well known funds that offer superior services and charge annual fees in the neighbourhood of one-fifth of the benchmark.[26] It may be argued that the small size of the Hong Kong market dictates that the rate must be high. However, one should recognize that investment activities today are highly internationalized. There is little difference between collecting funds in Hong Kong and in the United States. In any case, the money will have to be pooled.

The proper way to reduce costs is to rely on more competition. It is true that some elements of competition have already been built into the MPF plan. But if international fund houses find it hard to penetrate the market, this is not enough. Some people worry that allowing international competition will create too many schemes and that fees will be higher because of the lack of economies of scale. This is unlikely to happen. Competition will force those charging high fees to leave the market. Probably eventually only a few will remain. However, the potential for more efficient, new service providers to easily enter the market will prevent existing ones from imposing high fees or from behaving irresponsibly.

To increase competition, employees should not be deprived of their consumer choice. If they are the ones who make the decision about what scheme to join, it will be much harder for inferior service providers to survive. We should also not forget that the MPF is a compulsory scheme. As such, it has taken away part of the freedom of choice of the workers. It is inevitable that some inefficiencies will be created because of this. It is therefore all the more important to ensure that restrictions on free choice should be kept to a minimum. Five or six years after the MPF has begun operation the authority should probably review the policy once again.

Notes

1. See *World Development Report*, various issues, and *Hong Kong Annual Digest of Statistics 1997*.

2. *World Development Report 1997*, p. 225.

3. See *World Development Report 1997*, p. 215.

4. The world's average life expectancy at birth in 1995 was sixty-seven years.

5. See Hong Kong Government, Census and Statistics Department, *1996 Population By-Census-Summary Results*, p. 13.

6. Figures 5.1 and 5.2 are similar to the population pyramids commonly used in demographic analyses. However, for our purpose, we do not need to distinguish between males and females.

7. The benchmark projection of the population structure of 2036 in Table 5.1 is based on 1996 by-census data. In addition, I have made two assumptions. First, the age-specific birth and death rates of 1996 remain constant throughout the years. Second, there is no net inflow or outflow of immigrants. The first assumption tends to make the change in population structure less dramatic. The more likely scenario is that the death rate will continue to fall, meaning that there will be an even higher proportion of old people in the future. There is no indication that there will be a major reversal of the falling trend of the total fertility rate in the future. The second assumption is not realistic because there has indeed been an inflow of immigrants into Hong Kong. This has an important impact on the size of the population, but not necessarily on the population structure. Projections that take immigrants into account produce similar population patterns. Ageing of the population still occurs but is slowed down slightly.

8. Labour force participation rate is the proportion of working people in the population of a particular age cohort. Data on this are based on the Hong Kong Government's *Hong Kong Annual Digest of Statistics*, 1997. If we multiply the support ratio by the labour force participation rate, we get the number of taxpayers per retired person.

9. See Lui (1995) for a summary of some of the objections raised against the PAYG system in the Hong Kong context.

10. The calculations are based on several assumptions. The average real rate of growth of GDP is 4% a year before the PAYG system is imposed. After the reduction, it is 3.64%. Current GDP is HK$1,327 billion. The GDP figure is from the Hong Kong Government (1998).

11. See Hong Kong Government (1998).

12. See Lui (1997, chapter 17) for a detailed critique of the proposition that the co-existence of a PAYG scheme and a mandatory private pension fund is the optimal retirement-protection system for Hong Kong.

13. These public schemes can clearly be supplemented by private ones. For example, Keyfitz (1993) advocates that retirement age should be a choice variable controlled by the individual. If a person chooses to retire at a later age, she can enjoy a higher level of consumption during retirement.

14. The Hang Seng Index of April 1998 is about 110 times that of April 1964. The average annual rate of return should also take into account the dividends paid to the individual stocks, which average about 3.5% a year.

15. In more recent years, the rate of return of pension funds in the United States has generally gone up. For example, the largest pension fund in the United States, the College Retirement Equity Fund (CREF), has an average real rate of return of well over 10% a year for its stock account. See TIAA-CREF (1998).

16. This assumption is consistent with government statistics. The rate of increase in the salary, which is defined to include promotion or seniority increases, is indeed higher than is that of the wage rate, according to government statistics. See Hong Kong Government (1998).

17. It is not clear that the growth rate of the average wage rate can be as high as 2% a year. If the growth rate is lower, benefits from the PAYG system will also be lower.

18. Similar results can be obtained if we compare the computed internal rate of return of a PAYG system with the assumed rate of return of the MPF. Older or poorer people joining the PAYG system will enjoy a rate of return that is higher than that of the MPF.

19. I do not necessarily preclude the operation of other existing welfare programmes for the elderly. However, the one proposed here should form the core.

20. It is assumed that participants in the MPF can buy an actuarially fair annuity in the market. This provides the person with monthly payments until his death.

21. See Hong Kong Government, Social Welfare Department (1998) for detailed information on CSSA and other programmes.

22. Income figures and some population figures are from unpublished data of the Census and Statistics Department, Hong Kong Government.

23. The MPF benefit has been multiplied by a factor of 0.67 to reflect support for the nonworking spouse during retirement. This factor is the labour force participation rate for the adult population.

24. For more details on MPF schemes, see Hong Kong Government (1995), Hong Kong Government Provisional Legislative Council Bills Committee (1997a, 1997b, 1997c).

25. See Hong Kong Provisional Legislative Council Bills Committee (1997a, 1997b, 1997c) for details.

26. For example, see TIAA-CREF (1998).

CHAPTER 6

Concluding Remarks: The MPF after the Asian Financial Crisis

The rapid ageing of Hong Kong's population has made retirement protection one of the most critical social issues in the city. Indeed, the people of Hong Kong have not ignored it. For several decades they have debated about which retirement-protection system would be most suitable for them. This book reviews the history of the debates and offers explanations for the changes in government position. It also examines and analyzes the three most important options, namely, the pay-as-you-go (PAYG) system, the central provident fund (CPF), and the privately run mandatory provident fund (MPF). Understanding these three options is important in helping us make the right choice for Hong Kong.

The PAYG system is often politically attractive because some people in the current generation can gain as a result of it, even though it may cause future generations to lose. From an investment perspective, more people can gain if the population is becoming younger and younger over time. On the other hand, the system is not sustainable when the population is ageing quickly, because the outflow of funds will exceed the inflow. The PAYG scheme will likely reduce the long-run growth rate of an economy, especially when the latter is already well developed. Some of the alleged advantages of the system, such as fairness and a low risk level, upon closer scrutiny are demonstrated to be suspect. Experiences of countries that have employed the PAYG scheme, such as those of

Germany, the United States, China, and former members of the Soviet bloc, all include grappling with the difficulties inherent in the system.

The CPF is a forced-saving scheme. If such a plan is implemented in Hong Kong, the saving rate will likely go up in the short run, but it may drop back to the old level in the long run. It is not clear that the government can manage the fund at a lower cost than the private sector can. Empirical evidence shows that the CPF's rates of return are generally lower than those of private pension funds. The CPF is largely immune to the difficulties caused by changes in the demographic structure. In Singapore, which has the most successful CPF in the world, the theoretical disadvantages of the CPF are all present, but some have been mitigated in recent years by a series of liberalizing reforms that dilute the system. The particular political considerations for adopting the system in Singapore are not relevant to Hong Kong.

Chile has adopted a privately run pension system called the AFP. By issuing bonds to raise money, it was able to transit from the PAYG system to the AFP. After deducting for administrative costs, the average real rate of return of Chilean pension funds has remained very high. However, some deficiencies in the institutional design of the AFP have unnecessarily increased the administrative costs. The Chilean system also shares all of the drawbacks characteristic of a forced-saving scheme.

Which option should Hong Kong adopt? Is it necessary to adopt any option at all? The low fertility rate, high life expectancy, and relatively slow growth in real wage rate should preclude the consideration of a PAYG system. Total reliance on private initiatives to save in a pension plan is also problematic. It may very well be true that people belonging to the middle- and upper-income classes know how to save for their retirement. There is no need for the government to force them to do so. However, there could be moral hazard problems for the poorer group. Without a forced saving scheme, some people will fail to prepare for their retirement during their productive years. It will be very hard for the government to ignore destitute old people. Some people, realizing this, will fail to save when they are still young. Moreover, the accounts of a mandatory saving scheme are more transparent than ordinary private accounts. It will be harder for people to hide their accrued benefits when they must apply for supplementary welfare payments requiring a means test.

A mandatory saving scheme is suitable for Hong Kong, but by itself it is not sufficient. Some form of means-tested safety net for the low income group also has to be instituted.

A retirement plan for Hong Kong should be financially sustainable, simple and fair. The benefits should be sufficient to provide retirement protection. The recommendation is for the co-existence of a MPF and a means-tested welfare programme. Because of the ageing of the population, the government has to be concerned about the increasing cost of the welfare programme over time. However, accrued benefits from the MPF will go up as well. Simulation exercises show that the increasing trend of the latter will offset the former. If a welfare programme is properly implemented, it will be feasible for the government to ensure that welfare expenditures remain a constant share of the GDP, and, at the same time, that the total benefits of an individual from private pension and welfare receipts can adjust upwards according to the increase in wage income over time.

The Asian financial crisis that began to hit Hong Kong in 1997 has significantly changed the economic landscape of Hong Kong. Do the analyses in this book remain robust in light of recent events? Is it necessary to modify or abandon the MPF?

The PAYG system's fundamental difficulty is that it is unsustainable in the long run. Alternatively, if the tax rate does not go up over time, the implicit rate of return would be too low. Economic fluctuations like those caused by the Asian financial crisis cannot change the demographic structure in any significant way. They do not alleviate the PAYG system's problem. Moreover, the decline in the wage rate and the increase in unemployment also lower the monthly payments to the scheme.

The rate of return of the MPF will also be affected by the financial crisis. However, it is not clear whether the effect is positive or negative. If the crisis only exerts temporary effects, the resulting lowering of asset prices actually enables investors to buy at a cheap rate. If the effects are permanent, the long term growth rate of Hong Kong will decline. For reasons discussed in previous chapters, the implicit rate of return of the PAYG system will be hit hard. The long term rate of return for the MPF will also decline. However, since the MPF allows global diversification in the investment portfolio, the effects of a regional crisis will be less severe.

That it allows for global diversification is one of the advantages of the MPF. This is even more important in the aftermath of the Asian financial crisis. Without the pooling of funds made possible by the MPF, small investors would be less capable of avoiding losses as a result of the crisis. Their resources will more likely be locked in a declining market.

The weaknesses of the MPF are also more apparent in light of the crisis. As pointed out in Chapter 3, a forced-saving scheme like the MPF can create inefficiencies in resource allocation. People at different ages save for different purposes, but not necessarily for retirement. During a recession, saving may become an important precautionary insurance measure against unemployment. If we force people to put aside a large share of income to prepare for retirement, their ability to save for unemployment may be weakened. Fortunately, the MPF saving rate, which is equal to 10% of income, is only a small share of Hong Kong's voluntary gross domestic saving rate of 32%. The magnitude of the inefficiencies created, if any, will not be large. Moreover, the high voluntary rate means that a lot of savings must have been accumulated in the private sector over the years. This makes it easier for the people of Hong Kong to get through the rainy days.

Another consideration is that employers have to contribute 5% of wage income to the MPF on behalf of their workers. Some argue that this will pose additional costs for employers. In a time of recession, when there is a need to adjust wage incomes downwards, the MPF contributions may delay recovery. The validity of this argument is limited. Employers will view the 5% contribution as part of an employee's compensation package. If the market is sufficiently flexible, employers will cut wages by 5% once the MPF has been established. The problem mentioned above will not be important. However, if the labour market is rigid, then the introduction of the MPF in the midst of a recession will indeed delay recovery.

Is it necessary for the government to delay the implementation of the plan? The answer is no. The MPF brings many advantages to the Hong Kong people. A one-year delay could potentially cause a 10% reduction in the expected pension benefits for the future, because the foregone interests that will accrue will be very significant. Hong Kong's population is ageing rapidly. The earlier the MPF is implemented, the sooner Hong Kong will solve its retirement-protection problem. Moreover, a delay means that people with low income cannot take advantage of the MPF to diversify their portfolio. Most importantly, it will decrease the government's credibility. As shown in Chapter 1, the former colonial government in Hong Kong shifted its position too many times on retirement matters. After the change in sovereignty in 1997 there were often doubts as to whether the Hong Kong SAR Government would be able to stick to promises and policies committed to in the past. A very important reason for Hong Kong's previous economic success is the government's ability to follow fixed rules, rather than discretion, in formulating and implementing its budgetary policies.[1] It might cost the government's long-term credibility dearly to postpone a plan it painstakingly and rationally designed. The proper thing to do in light of the Asian financial crisis is to improve flexibility in the labour market. If the plan is implemented as it should be, there will be two years between the onset of the crisis and the actual launch of the MPF. This should be enough time for the labour market to make the proper wage adjustments. Delaying the implementation of the MPF is unnecessary.

Note

1. There are numerous examples suggesting that the government has often resorted to discretion rather than to rules in making recent decisions. Many commentators have pointed out that the Hong Kong Monetary

Authority's reliance on discretion has been important in inducing speculative attacks on the Hong Kong dollar. The government also appears willing to give up its announced plan of providing enough land each year to build 85,000 housing units. For the importance of following rules rather than discretion, see the classic article by Kydland and Prescott (1977).

Mathematical Appendix

The following shows how the expected contributions to the monthly pension payment can be calculated.

Let w = initial monthly wage rate,

α = proportion of wage income contributed to the forced saving scheme,

r = average real rate of return before retirement,

m = average growth rate of monthly wage,

n = length of working period (in number of months),

S = total sum accumulated for retirement.

Contribution in the first month is αw. Upon retirement this will become $\alpha w (1+r)^{n-1}$. Contribution in the second month is $\alpha w (1+m)$ and this will become $\alpha w (1+m)(1+r)^{n-1}$ upon retirement. By adding up these terms for every month from now to retirement, we get

$$S = \alpha w \left[(1+r)^{n-1} + (1+m)(1+r)^{n-2} + (1+m)^2(1+r)^{n-3} + \ldots + (1+m)^{n-1}\right]$$

$$= \alpha w \left[1+r\right]^{n-1} \left[\frac{1 - \left(\frac{1+m}{1+r}\right)^n}{1 - \left(\frac{1+m}{1+r}\right)}\right]. \tag{A-1}$$

In (A-1), it is assumed that $m < r$. Similar formulas can be derived for $m \geq r$.

Let P = real pension benefit per month,

K = number of months from retirement to death,

R = average real rate of return after retirement.

Since the present value of the future stream of pension benefits is equal to the total accumulated savings, we have,

$$P + \frac{P}{1+r} + \frac{P}{(1+r)^2} + \ldots + \frac{P}{(1+r)^{K-1}} = S \quad .$$

This is equivalent to

$$P = \left[\frac{1 - \left(\frac{1}{1+r}\right)}{1 - \left(\frac{1}{1+r}\right)^K} \right] S \quad . \tag{A-2}$$

Bibliography

1. Advisory Council on Social Security (1997). "Excerpts From the Report," *New York Times*, 7 January, p. A8.

2. Barro, Robert J. (1974). "Are Government Bonds Net Wealth?" *Journal of Political Economy*, Vol. 82: 1095–1118.

3. _____ (1978). *The Impact of Social Security on Private Saving: Evidence From the U.S. Time Series*. Washington, DC: American Enterprise Institute.

4. Batty, Iain (1997). "Mandatory Pension Funds in Hungary and Poland," *Benefits & Compensation International*, Vol. 27, No. 4: 2–7.

5. Becker, Gary, and Isaac Ehrlich (1994). "Social Security: Foreign Lessons," *The Asian Wall Street Journal*, 31 March.

6. Boskin, Michael J. (ed. 1977). *The Crisis in Social Security*. San Francisco: Institute for Contemporary Studies.

7. Campbell, G. Ricardo (1992). "Italian Social Security Reform," *Social Security Bulletin*, Vol. 55, No. 4 (winter): 69.

8. Case, Brendan M. (1998). "Mexico's Privatized Pension System Thriving," *Pensions & Investments*, Vol. 26, No. 2: 16, 22.

9. Castillo, Raul Bustos (1993). "Analysis of A National Private Pension Scheme: The Case of Chile — Comments," *International Labour Review*, Vol. 132, No. 3: 407–416.

10. Chan, Tonny (1994). "Pension Plan Body Blow," *Hong Kong Standard*, 1 September.

11. Cheung, Chor-yung (1995). Correspondence to Francis Lui, 17 August.

12. *China Statistical Yearbook* (1995). Beijing: China Statistical Publishing House.

13. Chow, Nelson (1994). "Old Age Pension Scheme — The Government's Wrong Choice," *Hong Kong Economic Journal*, 19 January (in Chinese).

14. Chow, Nelson (1996). "Ways of Financing Social Services for the Elderly," in *4th Annual Congress of Gerontology Abstract Book*, Hong Kong: Hong Kong Association of Gerontology.

15. Corsetti, Giancarlo, and Klaus Schmidt-Hebbel (1997). "Pension Reform and Growth," in *The Economics of Pensions: Principles*,

Policies, and International Experience, Salvador Valdes-Prieto, ed. New York: Cambridge University Press.

16. Diamond, Peter (1994). "Insulation of Pensions from Political Risk," *NBER Working Paper Series*, No. 4895, Cambridge, MA: NBER, Inc.

17. _____, and Salvador Valdes-Prieto (1994). "Social Security Reform," in *The Chilean Economy: Policy Lessons and Challenges*, Barry P. Bosworth, Rudiger Dornbusch, and Raul Laban, eds. Washington, DC: Brookings Institution.

18. Disney, Richard (1996). *Can We Afford To Grow Older?* Cambridge, MA.: MIT Press.

19. Ehrlich, Isaac, and Francis T. Lui (1991). "Intergenerational Trade, Longevity, and Economic Growth," *Journal of Political Economy*, Vol. 99: 1029–1059.

20. _____ (1997). "The Problem of Population and Growth: A Review of the Literature from Malthus to Contemporary Models of Endogenous Population and Endogenous Growth," *Journal of Economic Dynamics and Control*, Vol. 21: 205–242.

21. _____ (1998). "Social Insurance, the Family, and Economic Growth," *Economic Inquiry*, Vol. 36, No. 3 (July): 390–409.

22. Entwistle, R., and C. R. Winegarden (1984). "Fertility and Pension Programs in LDCs: A Model of Mutual Reinforcement," *Economic Development and Cultural Change*, Vol. 32: 331–354.

23. Esposito, Louis (1978). "Effect of Social Security on Saving: Review of the Studies Using U.S. Time Series Data," *Social Security Bulletin*, Vol. 41 (May): 9–17.

24. Fan, Zhuo Yun (1994). "Strategic Considerations of The Government's Sharp Turn in Retirement Protection Plan," *Hong Kong Economic Journal*, 12 January, p. 20 (in Chinese).

25. Feldstein, Martin S. (1974). "Social Security, Induced Retirement, and Aggregate Capital Accumulation," *Journal of Political Economy*, Vol. 82: 905–28.

26. _____ (1980). "International Differences in Social Security and Saving," *Journal of Public Economics*, Vol. 14: 225–44.

27. _____ (1995). "Social Security and Saving: New Time Series Evidence," *NBER Working Paper* No. 5054.

28. Fox, Louise (1994). "What To Do About Pensions in Transition Economies?" *Transition*, Vol. 5, No. 2–3, Research Department, World Bank.

29. Gillion, Colin, and Alejandro Bonilla (1992). "Analysis of A National Private Pension Scheme: The Case of Chile," *International Labour Review*, Vol. 131, No. 2: 171–195.

30. Hatta, Tatsuo, and Noriyoshi Oguchi (1997). "The Net Pension Debt of the Japanese Government," mimeographed, Institute of Social and Economic Research, Osaka University.

31. Hewitt Associates LLC and GML Consulting Ltd. (1995). *Report on the Mandatory Provident Funds System.* Hong Kong.

32. Hinchberger, Bill (1998). "Privatization Bolivia Style," *Institutional Investor*, Vol. 32, No. 1: 93–94.

33. *Hong Kong Commercial Daily*, various issues.

34. Hong Kong Economists (1994). "Our Objection To the Government Proposed Old Age Pension Scheme," *South China Morning Post*, 1 September, p. 14.

35. Hong Kong Government (1998). *Estimates of Gross Domestic Product 1961 to 1997.* Hong Kong Government Printer.

36. _____ (1995). "Mandatory Provident Fund Schemes Ordinance," *Ordinance No. 80 of 1995.*

37. _____. *Hong Kong Annual Digest of Statistics*, various issues. Hong Kong Government Printer.

38. _____. *Hong Kong Monthly Digest of Statistics*, various issues. Hong Kong Government Printer.

39. Hong Kong Government, Census and Statistics Department (1996). *1996 Population By-Census — Summary Results.* Hong Kong Government Printer.

40. Hong Kong Government, Education and Manpower Branch (1992). *A Community-Wide Retirement Protection System*, October.

41. _____ (1995). *Assessment of Public Opinion on the Consultation Paper "An Old Age Pension Scheme for Hong Kong,"* January.

42. _____ (1994). *Taking the Worry Out of Growing Old — An Old Age Pension Scheme for Hong Kong*, July.

43. Hong Kong Government, Social Welfare Department (1998). Homepage, http://www.info.gov.hk/swd/

44. Hong Kong Legislative Council (1991). "Central Provident Fund," *Hansard of the Sitting of the Legislative Council*, 10 July.

45. _____ (1993). "Retirement Protection," *Hansard of the Sitting of the Legislative Council*, 3 February.

46. Hong Kong Legislative Council (1995). "Retirement Protection," *Hansard of the Sitting of the Legislative Council*, 8 March.

47. Hong Kong, Provisional Legislative Council Bills Committee (1997a). "Total Picture on Security of Scheme Assets," *Provident Fund Schemes Legislation (Amendment) Bill 1997 Information Note*.

48. _____ (1997b). "Total Picture on Measures to Protect the Low-income Group," *Provident Fund Schemes Legislation (Amendment) Bill 1997 Information Note*.

49. _____ (1997c). "Total Picture on Measures to Minimize Administrative Costs," *Provident Fund Schemes Legislation (Amendment) Bill 1997 Information Note*.

50. *International Benefit Guidelines* (1989). New York: William M. Mercer International.

51. *International Labour Office* (1994). "Privatization of Pensions in Latin America," *International Labour Review*, Vol. 133, No. 1: 134–141.

52. Keyfitz, Nathan (1993). "The Retirement and Aging Problem of Social Security," *United Bulletin*, No. 48: 42–66.

53. Kielmas, Maria (1995). "Italy Passes Pension Reforms," *Business Insurance*, Vol. 29, No. 30: 17.

54. Kingston, Eric R. (1987). *What You Must Know About Social Security and Medicare*. New York: Pharos Books.

55. Kotlikoff, Laurence J. (1979). "Testing the Theory of Social Security and Life-Cycle Accumulation," *American Economic Review*, Vol. 69: 396–410.

56. _____ (1996). "Rescuing Social Security," *Challenge* (November–December) 21–22.

57. _____ and Jeffrey Sachs (1997). "The Personal Security System (PSS) — A Framework for Reforming Social Security," mimeographed.

58. Kritzer, Barbara (1993). "Sweden Reduces Social Security Costs," *Social Security Bulletin*, Vol. 56, No. 2 (summer): 93–4.

59. _____ (1996a). "Privatizing Social Security: The Chilean Experience," *Social Security Bulletin*, Vol. 59, No. 3 (fall): 45–55.

60. _____ (1996b). "Updates on Selected Latin America Countries," *Social Security Bulletin*, Vol. 59, No. 4 (winter): 75.

61. _____ (1997). "El Salvador to Offer Privatized Social Security," *Social Security Bulletin*, Vol. 60, No. 1: 63.

62. Kydland, Finn E., and Edward C. Prescott (1977). "Rules Rather Than Discretion: The Inconsistency of Optimal Plans," *Journal of Political Economy*, Vol. 85, June: 473–491.

63. Leimer, Dean, and Selig Lesnoy (1982). "Social Security and Private Saving: New Time Series Evidence," *Journal of Political Economy*, Vol. 90: 606–29.

64. Li, Wei Qiang (1994). "The Dream of Mandatory Private Retirement Protection System is Hard to Materialize," *Hong Kong Economic Journal*, 12 January, p. 20 (in Chinese).

65. Liberal Party (1994). *A Two-Pronged Proposal — Liberal Party Proposal on Retirement and Old Age Protection*. 2 October, Hong Kong.

66. Lin, Fu-de, and Lei Lu (1994). "*Di Sheng Yu Lu Xia Di Ren Kou Fa Zhan Qian Jing*" (Prospects of Population Development Under the Low Fertility Rate), *Ren Kou Yan Jiu* (Population Research), Vol. 18, No. 3 (May): 40–47.

67. Liu, Lilian (1991). "Social Security for State-Sector Workers in the People's Republic of China: The Reform Decade and Beyond," *Social Security Bulletin* (October), Vol. 54, No. 10: 2–16.

68. _____ (1993). "New Forms of Social Security in South China," *Social Security Bulletin* (Spring), Vol. 56, No. 1:93–94.

69. Loh, Christine (1993). "Retirement Protection," Correspondence to Francis Lui, 2 February.

70. Low, Linda (1996). "Central Provident Fund in Singapore," *HKCER Letters* (November), No. 41: 5–8.

71. Lucas Robert E., Jr. (1988). "The Mechanics of Economic Development," *Journal of Monetary Economics*, Vol. 22: 3–42.

72. Lui, Francis T. (1995). *Yong Jing Ji Xue Zuo Yan Jing* (Using Economics as Your Eyes), second edition. Hong Kong: Next Press (in Chinese).

73. _____ (1991). "Can the Government Substitute the Family? — The Social Loss of Mandatory Retirement Insurance for the Elderly," *HKCER Letters* (November), No. 11: 1–3.

74. _____ (1992). "On Retirement Protection in Hong Kong," *HKCER Letters* (November), No. 17: 1–2.

75. _____ (1994). "On Financial Viability of the Old Age Pension Scheme," *HKCER Letters* (March–July).

76. _____ (1997). *Feng Yan Zhong De Jing Ji Xue* (Economics at the Storm Eye). Hong Kong: Infowide Press (in Chinese).

77. *Ming Pao*, various issues.

78. Munnell, Alicia H. (1974). *The Effect of Social Security on Personal Saving*. Cambridge, MA: Ballinger.

79. Ng, Lilian (1993). "The Eighty Percent Solution," *Singapore Tatler* (July): 14–16.

80. Nugent , J. B. (1985) "The Old Age Security Motive for Fertility," *Population and Development Review*, Vol. 11: 75–98.

81. _____, and R. T. Gillaspy (1983). "Old Age Pensions and Fertility in Rural Areas of Less Developed Countries: Some Evidence from Mexico," *Economic Development and Cultural Change*, Vol. 31: 809–830.

82. One-Country-Two-Systems Economic Research Centre (1995). *An Individual-Based Mandatory Public and Private Provident Fund Scheme*. 23 May, Hong Kong.

83. OECD (1988). *Reforming Public Pensions*, Paris: OECD.

84. Russell, Francis (1973). "Bubble, Bubble — No Toil, No Trouble," *American Heritage Magazine, (February)*: 75–86.

85. Samuelson, Paul A. (1975). "Optimum Social Security in a Life-cycle Growth Model," *International Economic Review*, Vol. 16: 539–544.

86. Schulz, James H. (1988). *The Economics of Aging*, fourth edition. Dover, MA: Auburn House.

87. Schulz, James H. et al. (1974). *Providing Adequate Retirement Income: Pension Reform in the United States and Abroad*. Hanover, NH: University Press of New England.

88. Shum, Yat Fei (1994). "The Sincere Call of the Economists," *Kuai Bao (Express Daily)*, 15 September (in Chinese).

89. Singapore, Central Provident Fund Board. *Annual Report*, various years.

90. Singapore, Department of Statistics (1995). *Yearbook of Statistics*.

91. *Social Security Bulletin* (1993). *Annual Statistical Supplement*.

92. Solow, Robert (1956). "A Contribution to the Theory of Economic Growth," *Quarterly Journal of Economics*, Vol. 81: 65–94.

93. *South China Morning Post*, various issues.

94. Steinmeyer, Heinz-Dietrich (1991). "Federal Republic of Germany," in *International Handbook of Old-Age Insurance*, Martin B. Tracy and Fred C. Pampel, eds. New York: Greenwood Press.

95. Tay, Boon Nga (1992). "The Central Provident Fund: Operation and Schemes," in *Public Policies in Singapore: Changes in the 1980s and*

Future Signposts, Linda Low and Toh Mun Heng, eds. Singapore: Times Academic Press.

96. TIAA–CREF (1998). *TIAA–CREF Homepage, http://www.tiaa.org/*

97. Tsang, Donald (1997). Speech at the Opening Ceremony of Far Eastern Meeting of Econometric Society Symposium on "Growing into 21st Century: Hong Kong, China and Asia-Pacific," 25 July.

98. United States Government (1996). *Statistical Abstracts of the United States*. Washington, DC: U.S. Government Printer.

99. Van der Noord, Paul, and Richard Herd (1993). "Pension Liabilities in the Seven Major Economies," *OECD Economics Dept. Working Paper*. Paris.

100. Vittas, Dimitri (1995). "Pension Funds and Capital Markets," *Working Paper*, World Bank, Policy Research Dept., Washington, DC.

101. _____, and Augusto Iglesias (1992). "The Rationale and Performance of Personal Pension Plans in Chile," *Policy Research Working Paper 867*, World Bank, Financial Sector Development Dept., Washington, DC.

102. Williamson, John B., and Fred Pampel (1993). *Old-Age Security in Comparative Perspective.*, New York: Oxford University Press.

103. Willis, J. A. (1995). "Retirement Protection," *Correspondence to Francis Lui*, 6 March.

104. Wong, Richard (1993). "Lessons of the Singapore Central Provident Fund," *HKCER Letters* (September), No. 22: 6–8.

105. World Bank (1994). *Averting the Old Age Crisis*. New York: Oxford University Press.

106. _____ (1996a). *"China — Pension System Reform,"* China and Mongolia Department, Report No. 15121–CHA.

107. _____ (1996b). *World Development Report 1996*. New York: Oxford University Press.

108. _____ (1997a). *World Development Report 1997*. New York: Oxford University Press.

109. _____ (1997b). *Old Age Security — Pension Reform in China*. Washington, DC: World Bank.

110. Wyatt Company (HK) Ltd. (1995). *Wyatt 1994 Annual Report: Measurement of Investment Performance Survey for Hong Kong Retirement Schemes.*

Index

About the Author

Francis T. Lui is Director of the Center for Economic Development, The Hong Kong University of Science and Technology. He holds bachelor and doctoral degrees in economics from the University of Chicago and the University of Minnesota, respectively. Before joining the University of Science and Technology as a founding faculty member in 1991, he was associate professor of economics at the State University of New York at Buffalo.

Author and editor of six books on economic issues in Hong Kong and China, he has published numerous articles in leading international journals. In recent years, he has developed a second career as an economic commentator and popular writer. Professor Lui is a member of the Task Force on Employment of the Hong Kong SAR Government, and his opinions are frequently sought by the local and international media, business organizations, political parties and the government.

The Hong Kong Economic Policy Studies Series